Discipleship
and the
Evangelical Church

Discipleship
and the
Evangelical Church

A Critical Assessment

JESSE HAMILTON

WIPF *&* STOCK · Eugene, Oregon

DISCIPLESHIP AND THE EVANGELICAL CHURCH
A Critical Assessment

Copyright © 2022 Jesse Hamilton. All rights reserved. Except for brief quotations in critical publications or reviews, no part of this book may be reproduced in any manner without prior written permission from the publisher. Write: Permissions, Wipf and Stock Publishers, 199 W. 8th Ave., Suite 3, Eugene, OR 97401.

Wipf & Stock
An Imprint of Wipf and Stock Publishers
199 W. 8th Ave., Suite 3
Eugene, OR 97401

www.wipfandstock.com

PAPERBACK ISBN: 978-1-6667-3481-2
HARDCOVER ISBN: 978-1-6667-9115-0
EBOOK ISBN: 978-1-6667-9116-7

02/08/22

Scripture quotations marked (NASB) are taken from the (NASB®) New American Standard Bible®, Copyright © 1960, 1971, 1977, 1995, 2020 by The Lockman Foundation. Used by permission. All rights reserved. www.lockman.org

Resident Aliens quoted by permission from Abingdon Press

Gospel quoted by permission from Lifeway Press

For Lizzy

may you never forget
and strive always to live out
the message of this book

Contents

Acknowledgements | ix
Introduction | xi

1. The Gospel | 1
2. Holiness | 25
3. Prayer and the Holy Spirit | 54
4. Mission | 80
5. Idols | 103
6. Causes | 130
7. The Way Forward | 151

Bibliography | 169

Acknowledgements

THERE HAVE BEEN so many influences, friendships, and conversations that have played a significant part in the formation of this book; it would be impossible to acknowledge everyone. Special thanks goes to my wife, Ana, who patiently read and commented on the manuscript along the way, providing numerous helpful suggestions. My gratitude as well to Matthew J. Hart for his helpful comments on chapters 1, 2, and 4.

Introduction

REMEMBER THAT SCENE AT the end of *Schindler's List* when the title character breaks down weeping because he wanted to save "one more person?" That was me in 2003. It was a needy, developing country in Asia, and I was a young, failed missionary. I wasn't *really* a missionary, in the biblical sense of the term; I had come to Asia after college to work with my parents because I felt burdened to give up my life for the cause of Christ, and sure, God had used me in some ways, but I wasn't a true missionary—even though I thought I was at the time. I was, however, a *failure*, in a very real sense; or at least I felt so. I was still lazy after God, not spending nearly enough time in his Word and prayer—especially prayer—to be consistently useful; and as a young, single man still struggling with significant maturity issues, I was easy pickings for Satan, especially in a spiritual war zone. After four years of up-and-down usefulness, I was returning home for my brother's wedding, but I knew I needed to come off the field for a while and regroup. It was fully my decision, but it was agonizingly difficult to make. As I knelt in my little bedroom apartment for the final time before driving to the airport, I began to weep. Regret overwhelmed me; my sobs were deep and real. How many more eternal souls could God have used me to rescue? Why hadn't I been able to overcome my weaknesses for matters of eternal significance? Why hadn't I been able to build on all that I had learned and experienced, all the blessings that God had poured into my life?

My parents stayed on, and God graciously continued to pour out his Spirit on their ministry, which had an impact all throughout the region; and later, when the government kicked them out of the country they were in, they continued working in other needy areas in Asia, where they remain today. I returned home, did an internship in a local church, met and married my wife, and started teaching school, one of the few jobs available to someone with only an English degree. Before long, my wife and I started to get that itch again, and in a matter of time, with the blessing of my parents, pastors, and other spiritual advisors, we were back on the field in Asia. It was an incredible blessing of God to be able to return. And this time, I felt sure, it would be a permanent move.

Things began wonderfully. God was using us in local universities and in our parents' work, and we even had our only child there, a daughter. Though we had no financial support from home, God was blessing us in obvious ways. I was older, spiritually stronger, and better prepared. I knew what I was getting into, and I was ready for an increasingly meaningful ministry. There was nothing more I wanted to do with my life; I was living my dream, the dream I had carried since I was seven years old. I still remember those early years, when my father, then a pastor, preached urgently and often about the needs of the world and the priority of missions. I determined then and there that I would heed the call; after all, if I didn't do it, who would? After becoming a Christian in my late teens, I gave up serious interest in intellectual pursuits, especially philosophy, to major in English in college so that I could teach it overseas and thereby get a visa, and by graduation, I was ready to go. Sure, I wasn't quite prepared the first go-round, but God had graciously placed me on the field once again, and this time, it was for keeps.

Only it wasn't. Three years in, my wife, an enormously talented classical pianist who had come to the States from Europe to study piano, was shocked to find that her American green card, which we knew was expiring but which we were told could be renewed overseas, in fact only could be renewed in the States. By the time that information was confirmed the green card had expired. The result was that she could no longer live in the United States, not only my home country but the country where her entire family had immigrated, unless she reapplied for an immigrant visa–from Asia. After a few somewhat panicked weeks of prayer, our choice became clear. Unless we wanted the situation to turn into a serious, long-term quandary, we would have to restart the immigration process. And, clearly, we would need to stay in the States until my wife became a United States citizen. As the reality began to sink in, so did the discouragement. Once again, it seemed, I would have to leave the field and return home—not as a failure this time, but with tremendous disappointment nonetheless, to face and to do who knew what.

Within a month of that decision the drama was largely over. My wife had graciously been granted an immigration visa from Asia, and we found ourselves back in the States, teaching (yet again) at a Christian school and trying to make a living for ourselves and our young family. But what we thought was going to take three years of waiting has now taken twelve. My wife got her American citizenship, but then our daughter was diagnosed with scoliosis—nothing life-threatening, thankfully, but serious enough to need constant, vigilant care for a number of years, to try and avoid major surgery until she stops growing. Over the past decade, God has graciously provided all of our needs, my wife and I have obtained postgraduate degrees, and we have known useful ministry opportunities, but if we were honest, living and working in the United States has been almost overwhelmingly depressing. To put it bluntly, while America is more secular and needy than ever before, and the need for evangelism and discipleship real and acute, we remain convinced that most people here have more spiritual truth and opportunity available to them in a day than whole people groups in other countries have in a lifetime. The gap in spiritual knowledge and possibilities between America and many parts of the world is still not even close. Furthermore, America has had its chances, while there are still many countries where the gospel has not been clearly proclaimed. And there are burgeoning discipleship needs in every developing country where the gospel has known success. America is getting worse, to be sure, but America is still one of the last countries on earth that a missionary needs to prioritize, just in terms of spiritual light. And yet here we are, ministering to young people who know more than whole people groups do, doing things that seemingly any Christian could, even those with no theological training and little maturity. Only God could do something like this. And only God can help us survive it.

So why this book? It's simple. I've learned lessons overseas, no doubt, but I've learned even more after coming home. I've experienced a wide swath of Christian culture. As I've moved from job to job, I've spent a large amount of time in various churches. And what I've learned has been fascinating and encouraging at times, but also sobering and downright disconcerting. And then, of course, the pandemic hit, and boy, did that show the world what the Evangelical church was made of. The upshot of it all is that despite the many books on discipleship that appear every year, many of which are percipient and undeniably useful, my misgivings about writing books and similar endeavors, which I will discuss later, and the many good things in the Evangelical church that we should be thankful for, there is, in my opinion, much that yet needs to be reexamined, repented of, and recalibrated. In fact, I believe the situation in the American Evangelical church to be far more urgent than many realize. There is talk of an impending crisis in some Evangelical denominations; but the real problems, in my view, remain largely unexplored. In this book, I hope to address these issues as carefully as I can, and hopefully provide some scriptural guidance about the way forward. In the end, though, my contention will be that what I have set forth is neither radical nor unattainable; it is simply ordinary Christianity, the basic Christian life we are all called to in the New Testament.

First, though, some disclaimers. For one thing, as I have hinted, I am an Evangelical Protestant, and thus my remarks will be intended most specifically, of course, for the Evangelical Protestant church. Second, my theology is unapologetically Reformed. Most of my reading, thinking, and learning over the years, especially in graduate school, has centered on critical questions of theology and philosophy related to the nature of man, especially the question of man's will, or free will in general. And to state it succinctly, nothing in all my reading and learning has dissuaded me of my Reformed convictions; they have only strengthened them. But why would I mention this somewhat inflammatory claim here? As will no doubt become clear, the full significance and impact of much of what I will discuss will depend, to some degree, on the extent to which the Reformed perspective is understood and embraced. Nevertheless, I would greatly hope that those from other doctrinal perspectives can benefit from what I write, and I work hard at key points in the book to ensure that indeed they can.

Another disclaimer is that I am not, in fact, a comfortable practical writer. My graduate training was in philosophical theology and analytic philosophy, the areas in which I am most comfortable researching and writing. I hope these realities will not be too much of a hindrance. Perhaps more to the point, in a book of this sort, where an attempt must be made to reach the largest possible audience, some degree of compromise must be sought regarding the detail and rigor one sets forth in support of one's claims. There will be times, no doubt, when some readers will think adequate theological defense, depth, and rigor are lacking; there will be others who think the discussion too tedious. In the end, I can only hope that sufficient biblical support is provided for the Holy Spirit to do his work, without weighing down the minds and attention spans of those who might also benefit from this book.

Finally, and most importantly: much of what I write here will be real, raw, and at times tough to read. This is a necessary part of any critical inquiry and of self-examination; nevertheless, my aim is to present all things in a spirit of humility, gentleness, and love. I hope and pray that this comes across as you read this book. Some things will be tough to consider, to be sure; but these are difficult and incredibly dangerous times. Real talk is needed. Furthermore, I wish to make it clear that I, as much or more than anyone, need repentance and growth in all of the areas that I will discuss. The lessons I have learned above any others, after all, are those that pertain to my own sin and my own need for sanctification. What we all need in these matters is scriptural honesty and a humble and contrite spirit.

Whatever here is true and needed, may God ignite by the flame of his Holy Spirit in the depths of our souls. Such power is, after all, our only hope.

1

The Gospel

My wife Ana (pronounced Ah-na in the Russian language) is an endlessly fascinating person. Born in the Soviet Union in the early eighties, she grew up in the tiny country of Moldova, which gained independence after the Soviet Union's collapse. The changes brought about after the decline of the Soviet communist bloc plunged her home country into widespread poverty. She grew up genuinely poor. Her parents often had to take odd jobs just to help the children survive, even serving as missionaries in outer Siberia for several years to make ends meet. She received charity packages from the West, wore hand-me-downs from her *brother*, and worked with her family every autumn to prepare preserves to get them through the winter. Life was hard—but glorious in its own right. Her parents, both incredibly talented and accomplished musicians, worked hard to foster an intellectual environment in the family. Ana grew up reading Pushkin, Dostoevsky, and translations of Shakespeare, while immersing herself in all the glorious music of the western classical tradition. The talents and musical legacy of her parents were passed on to each of the four children, but in none did they find more magnificent expression than in Ana, who by an early age was something of a local celebrity, showcasing her prodigious piano talents on national television and in numerous competitions. By the time she was in high school, her parents had shipped her off to boarding school in Romania, where the environment and teaching at the time were better suited to develop her world-class piano talent. Despite the horrors of living in a foreign country, and one that was at times hostile to her Moldavian heritage, Ana continued to progress as a concert pianist, winning more and more competitions and making plans to study abroad in a more developed country.

Toward the end of her senior year in high school, Ana heard of a once-in-a-lifetime opportunity: a famed Moldavian concert pianist, known throughout the world as one of the greatest living pianists, was returning home to perform and host auditions for a new piano department he was creating in, of all places, a small college in the States near my hometown, where he hoped possibly to retire. When Ana was informed of this thrilling piece of news, she was a country away in Romania, still grinding away at her studies. Somehow she managed to hop on a train, travel all night to Moldova, and make it in time for the pianist's auditions, which were to take place before his concert. When her time finally came to play for him, the unthinkable happened—the lights in the auditorium went completely out. Still in the midst of Liszt's dramatic but treacherous transcendental etude no. 12 ("Snowstorm"), Ana played on, and when she finished, the great pianist sat in perfect silence for a minute or two in the near total darkness. When he finally spoke, it was to ask if she had a passport. Afterward, Ana found evidence to suggest that a jealous parent of a fellow auditioner had switched off the lights in an effort to sabotage her performance. But it was no matter. God was bringing Ana to my hometown—and, eventually, through another set of remarkable providences, to my home church. And there, before her senior year of college, I was to meet her.

When I met Ana she was again something of a local celebrity, having won important competitions in Louisiana and in the southeastern United States, and having been well on her way for some time to what appeared for all the world to be a successful and even illustrious concert pianist career. Her mentor had been fashioning what was to become one of the great piano departments of the South in its heyday, and Ana was something of its prize jewel. But unbeknownst to me at the time I met her, God had already set the wheels of change into motion. Just before Ana and I met, her world-renowned, enormously gifted mentor had rather shockingly not been rehired. What appeared to be a clear future path for Ana was now covered by brambles of confusion. Or not, actually. Even before her mentor's departure, the Holy Spirit had been speaking to Ana in that still, small voice, unmistakable in its faith-fueled luminescence. How could she continue to spend hour upon hour in a tiny practice room, wasting away her life for the lure of the concert stage? Especially with so many needs in the world? In the end, as she tells it, it was the simple demand of Jesus to save one's life by losing it that carried the day. The fame, fortune, glamour, and even the deep and abiding beauty of the music she played and the artistry she demonstrated while playing it—nothing was going to keep her from fully following Jesus. By the time I met her, her decision had already been made. The departure of her mentor, in the end, was a catalyst of sorts, but it was also merely confirmation of where the Lord was already leading her. She was going to Africa to work with needy, unevangelized children—unless I, fresh from my first stint overseas, could persuade her to consider the part of the world I had been working in. Thank God I eventually did.

We had a glorious senior year together, attending all of her fabulous concerts and recitals, some solo, some with orchestra. As I traveled with Ana to each and every venue dressed in my concert best—my only suit—with the dazzling star of the hour upon my arm, who was now my fiancé, I got a glimpse of a world I had always dreamed of—a world not merely of elegance and sophistication, but one of undeniable, divinely-charged beauty. Night after night, midst an atmosphere of splendor, I was whisked away into the intoxicating fantasy-worlds of Rachmaninoff, Liszt, and whomever else my wife was playing. It was heady stuff—and mercifully short-lived. As soon as we were married it abruptly ended. My wife and I were plunged headlong into the world of what it means to follow Jesus—where circumstances are often uncertain, faith tested, provision delayed, requests sought for and miraculously provided, and God's grace desperately depended on through the means of prayer. And in this world we have remained for the past nearly two decades.

The secular world, and even parts of the Christian world, would say Ana made an incomprehensible mistake. She would counter with the simple claim that is at the heart of this chapter: to follow Jesus means to give up *everything*. I am not convinced that the Evangelical church today really understands what this means.

RECENT TRENDS

I want to begin our consideration of the foundational truths of the Christian faith—what the New Testament calls the gospel—by examining a recent trend. The "gospel-centered" movement has become quite influential in the Evangelical Protestant church of late, and its proponents have been earnest in their intention to make the gospel not merely the entry point of the Christian faith, but also the focal point and even the substance of the faith, as is often said in such churches. A well-known advocate puts it like this:

> Growth in Christ is not going beyond the gospel, but deeper into it. Believing the gospel is what released an explosive power in Jesus' followers that caused them to live with radical recklessness and audacious faith. Make the gospel the center of your life. Turn to it when you are in pain. Let it be the foundation of your identity. Ground your confidence in it. Run to it when your soul feels restless. Take solace there in times of confusion and comfort there in times of regret. Dwell on it until righteous passions for God spring up with in you. Let it inspire you to God-centered, death-defying dreams for His glory . . . Study it, deeply—like the seminarian studies doctrine, but like you study a sunset that leaves you speechless; or like a man who is passionately in love with his wife studies her, until he's so captivated by her that his enthrallment with her drives out any allurements toward other women. The gospel is not merely the diving board off of which you jumped into the pool of Christianity; the gospel is the pool itself. So keep going deeper into it. You'll never find the bottom.[1]

Having spent considerable time in such churches over the past many years, I can testify to the zeal with which this enterprise is carried out. To be sure, there were many in one church I attended, which was fairly large and influential in that part of the country, who appeared conflicted about the terminology at times; in the back rooms where various ministries were taking place, some of which I had the privilege to be a part of for a couple of years, the leader of one particular ministry repeatedly substituted the term "God-centered" for "gospel-centered"—almost instinctively—and the exchange was met from time to time with murmurs of approval.

It is not my intention to explore this matter extensively in this book; my general purpose lies elsewhere. However, since this trend has captivated so many around the country, and the movement has gained so much momentum, and since my larger purpose is to point out those issues in the church which, I believe, need to have the light of examination

---

1. Greear, *Gospel*, 245–46.

The Gospel

shined on them anew, it would be useful to make at least one or two comments in passing, despite the fact that many have offered substantial criticisms of this movement in recent years.

First, very generally, surely one must be incredibly careful with terminology, especially when it enters widespread usage or popularity. When such phrases as "gospel-centered" begin to grow in prominence, it is virtually inevitable that some vital aspect of biblical doctrine—or even some aspect of the subject itself—goes missing. After spending several years in one church that was quite large and incredibly influential, I can tell you that the phrase did, in fact, begin to take on a significance whose parameters were a bid too wide. It was mentioned without fail in every service, it seemed, and eventually it was presented as the sum total and substance of everything one needs to know in order to become more like Jesus, as the quote above makes explicit. A favorite verse was 1 Corinthians 15:3: "For I delivered to you as of first importance what I also received, that Christ died for our sins according to the Scriptures." A brief study of this verse reveals that the precise meaning of the phrase often rendered in English translations as "of first importance" is anything but certain; but the point here is that "of *first* importance," even if this is the proper translation, in a very real sense became "of *sole* importance." Despite the benefit of consistently focusing on the gospel, I found that the resulting problems were twofold: a general neglect of the larger set of vital biblical doctrines that the New Testament writers obviously thought essential to our sanctification, and an inadequate view of the grace of God, one that lent itself to abuse. This latter problem was especially acute, as young Christian friends I knew battled with remaining sin, assurance, and the like, and were constantly bombarded by the lure of what at times smacked of "cheap grace," as Bonhoeffer famously put it.[2] I believe, as Bonhoeffer did in his day, that an honest study of the New Testament makes it clear that the way the gospel is presented today is often unbiblical, for lack of a better term, as it fails to capture various nuances of the Christian message as presented in both the gospels and the epistles. Simply put, an emphasis on the forgiveness of our sins in Christ to the neglect of, say, the necessity of holiness, is simply not the way the Christian faith and life are presented in the New Testament. But more on this later.

My primary critique of this movement is as follows: how or why we should "center" our lives on anything other than the *actual* center of

---

2. Bonhoeffer, *Discipleship*, 43.

the universe, God himself, is difficult to apprehend. The reason the term "God-centered" resonated a bit more with my ministry-leader friend, perhaps, is because it simply makes more sense to say it, logically and biblically. The gospel is not bigger than God himself. On the Christian worldview, logically-speaking, God is clearly at the center of the universe, however one wishes to define the term "center"; and the Bible certainly places him there. As Romans 11:36 puts it, all things emanate from him, are achieved through him, and are unto him, or for his glory. And the fact that this particular verse comes at the end of an extended passage in which God's sovereignty over all things, even over the salvation of individuals and the destiny of entire people groups, is unapologetically proclaimed, underscores, I believe, the legitimate scope and utility of the term "God-centered."

Furthermore, what the term "gospel-centered" could indicate, to outsiders, is an intentional shift in emphasis or focus. Might use of the term "gospel-centered" be intended by some to imply a move away from the "austere" Reformed notion of the God-centeredness of God, i.e., that he does everything for his own glory, and that not only redemption, but also the demonstration of his perfect justice in the punishment of sinners, is part of his ultimate aim? I would argue that to the degree that it does indicate such an intentional shift, to that degree it must be rejected. Again, no zeal for the theological notions of grace, mercy, redemption, mission, or, for that matter, the philosophical notion of free will,[3] are biblically or logically robust enough to challenge the status of the God-centeredness of God as the ultimate explanation for the existence of the universe and all things in it. And to this end, as I will claim throughout this book, we must constantly direct ourselves.

Certainly, if defenders of "gospel-centered" thinking wish to counter by arguing that the term is meant to correct an emphasis on God's sovereignty, or on various other doctrines, *to the neglect of* the gospel, then this, I would argue, might be a helpful corrective in some instances. There is little doubt that many Reformed congregations in the later twentieth century, and I am thinking here especially of those who hold to the Westminster or London Baptist confessions, have had a tendency to "reform" to the point of missing critical elements of New Testament practical theology. The neglect of a "gospel" or "missional" culture in such churches

---

3. I remain convinced that a serious conviction of the sovereignty of God over all evil is an essential element of any workable theodicy—for both theological and philosophical reasons.

has undoubtedly been real, as has, perhaps, a lack of emphasis on God's grace and mercy. Having grown up in such contexts, I have witnessed it firsthand. Reminding ourselves consistently of the significance of God's grace, mercy, and forgiveness in the gospel is surely paramount; as is the need to be on the front lines of God's kingdom, which comes in the world through the preaching of the gospel to sinners, persistent prayer, and care for the needy and oppressed. Nevertheless, in my view the need for caution regarding the use of such terminology holds. Just as, in the end, the term "God-centered" was perhaps overemphasized by a-bit-too-zealous adherents of Calvinist theology, so too has the term "gospel-centered" suffered the same fate. Certainly, as we will see, being faithful to the mission of the church requires us never to stray too far from the gospel message and a gospel purpose. But there is always a tendency to overreact and go too far to the other side. In short: there is simply no substitute for preaching the "whole counsel of God," in as balanced a way as possible, and letting Scripture speak for itself. We must always be wary of slogans and trends; dangerous imbalances may be lurking.

NOT-SO-SUBTLE HERESIES

Another issue we should at least touch on is the question of the purity of the gospel. Many of us are now all-too-familiar with the movement known as the New Perspective, which seeks to cast doubt on the understanding of the gospel that was recovered and proclaimed during the Protestant Reformation. Among other things, New Perspective writers' aim was to show that when it comes to salvation, and in particular justification, the apostle Paul especially is interested less in one's individual standing before God, and more in one's relationship to the community of God's people; also, flowing out from this point, when Paul speaks of "works," he means merely to denote attempts by Jews to establish their own ethnic identity (in things like circumcision and the like), which leads to a newfound appreciation of the larger role of works in the matter of justification.[4]

It is certainly beyond the aim of this book to address these issues to any degree of depth; neither do I possess, perhaps, the exegetical training

---

4. This somewhat simplistic presentation of the New Perspective is adapted from Douglas Moo's overview in *Justification and Variegated Nomism*; see Moo, "Israel and the Law," 186–87.

to do so. Nevertheless, suffice it to say, I believe it to be abundantly clear to any honest student of the Scriptures that neither of the above claims of the New Perspective hold up under scrutiny. As multiple Evangelical scholars have shown, though there certainly is a communal aspect to salvation, in the sense that justified souls are brought into fellowship with the people of God, it is abundantly clear throughout the New Testament that this sense is secondary to the matter of one's individual relationship to God. I would even argue that this is quite obviously the case from the Scriptures. Furthermore, regarding the second point, although there can be no doubt that New Perspective writers have shed light on some issues that are often neglected, such as the reality of a final justification, in which all believers will stand before God and give an account for their lives, in no sense does this overturn or outweigh the overwhelming contention in the New Testament that justification and salvation are matters of *faith*—that to be justified, one must believe and trust solely in the righteousness put forward by God, the righteousness found in the person and work of Jesus Christ.

It is therefore a matter of great encouragement that Evangelical pastors and scholars have worked and fought hard to overturn the challenges of the New Perspective, and that the truths of the gospel have been preserved in the church. Again, like any earnest critical inquiry, the New Perspective shed light on a handful of things that the church has greatly benefitted from reexamining. But the truths that the Holy Spirit powerfully reestablished in the church during the Reformation stand unfazed. These, then, we assert as the plain facts of the gospel: humanity, afflicted by the disease of sin, stands condemned *en masse*, and is both in need of forgiveness and utterly insufficient to provide it. Atonement for sin, and the appeasement of God's wrath, have been provided by God himself, in the person of his own Son, Jesus, who came as a morally perfect sacrifice to die, as the lamb of God prefigured in the Old Covenant community who takes away the sin of the world. To receive the blessings of forgiveness, and be reconciled to God—and, indeed, be made part of the community of the saints—one must not hope in, appeal to, or otherwise depend on one's own righteousness or works, but rather must believe in, trust in, put their faith in, accept, and depend fully on the righteousness provided by God; in short, they must put their faith in Jesus and what he has done. Justification is not, as some in the New Perspective camp have attempted to claim, mere assent to the reality that Jesus is Lord; it is, rather, a casting of one's entire hope upon Jesus as savior, with all of the merits of that role that only Jesus can embody.

Yet the reality that this profound concept of faith can easily be abused has long been acknowledged in the modern church. Since the twentieth century, works such as Bonhoeffer's *The Cost of Discipleship* all the way down to John MacArthur's *The Gospel According to Jesus* have noted the tendency of the modern church to make grace and forgiveness too casual and easy a thing. Thus, in setting forth the gospel as we have, we would do well to point, along with these authors and a host of others, to the fact that wherever the gospel has been preached, from Jesus in the very beginning to the book of Revelation, the notion of repentance has been an inseparable component, so inextricably tied to the gospel that it can rightly be said to be an essential aspect of it. "The time is fulfilled, and the kingdom of God is at hand; repent and believe in the gospel" are the first recorded words of our Lord Jesus in the gospel of Mark (1:15), believed by many scholars to be the earliest account of the life of Jesus to be written down. Here, repentance is clearly presented as a command to all souls everywhere; it is the foundational duty proclaimed upon the inauguration of the kingdom of God in the world. In the book of Revelation, which contains our Lord's final message to the church, the command to repent is repeated so often that it only needs to be underscored how clearly and definitively repentance is reaffirmed as a duty commanded of all souls everywhere. No soul can be justified, or saved, without repentance from their sins. Nor do we need to go into great detail to defend repentance from being a work, or something by which a soul may gain merit; repentance in the Bible is a humbling, a sense of sorrow, a recognition of one's failures and need for forgiveness, and a posture of utter and complete receptivity to the will of God; all of these connotations are clearly bound up in the word itself. We can therefore demand repentance and make it an essential element of the call of God to salvation, as explicitly mentioned in Acts 20:21 and Hebrews 6:1, without need for elaborate defense of the purity of faith. To not repent is to fail to recognize one's sinfulness and need of a savior. To not repent is, in essence, to refuse to receive salvation. Repentance, then, is a *sine qua non*, or essential element, not just of the gospel message, but of faith itself.

But back to the problem made much of by some New Perspective authors: what do we make of passages that appeal to a final justification by works? I see no conflict here; God's intention has always been to make us holy, not just "legally" in justification, but actually, in sanctification.

"You shall be holy, for I am holy" is a command that stretches the length of the biblical record. Furthermore, it is clear that God's intention is to make us actually holy before we enter into his heavenly kingdom (Heb 12:14). Let us make no mistake: it is not the will of God to justify someone without sanctifying them. God's purpose, culminated in heaven, is to restore us to that level of blamelessness we had before sin entered the world. Holiness, then, is as essential a requirement for entrance into God's kingdom, a *sine qua non,* as repentance is. "God is not mocked," Paul warns us in Galatians 6:7. It is those who sow according to the Spirit who will reap eternal life.

Again, however, we must never make holiness the *ground*, or basis, of our justification or of our salvation. Some New Perspective writers have attempted to fully separate these two notions, and claim that while faith *justifies* us, it is our works that will finally *save* us on the last day. And while there are passages in the New Testament, of course, in which these are presented as two distinct realities or events, the idea that one has to do with faith while the other involves works is simply wrong. The Bible's declaration that we are unable to improve our situation, due to our corruption by sin and being under the penalty of God's wrath, holds. We must have the righteousness of God to be saved, and not our own, so that no one may boast, Paul tells us repeatedly. Furthermore, as verses such as Romans 5:9 make absolutely clear, justification *guarantees* our salvation from God's wrath. And some passages tell us explicitly that even our *salvation* by faith is guaranteed: by grace, through faith, we *have been saved*, Ephesians 2:8 tells us. Nor should we ever hold, as the Catholics and some other denominations do, that justification is a joint effort between God and man; or that works somehow play a part in our salvation, if those works are produced by the Spirit of God, and not ourselves. All such thinking is wrong. Though some of the biblical evidence is difficult to reconcile at times, we must simply acknowledge that the Bible is clear, powerfully so, on how we are justified, and it is clear as well that this justification by faith ensures that we will be saved (Rom 5:1, 8:30; Titus 3:7). Nevertheless, it is also clear that it is God's will to make us holy, that we should pursue this holiness with all our might, and that without it, we will not enter into heaven.

Again, there is no real problem here, no contradiction, as one might say in an introductory logic class. One statement, the affirmation of *sola fide*, is the following:

> (1) If a soul is justified, it is justified by faith alone.

The negation of this statement would obviously be the following:

> (2) It is not the case that if a soul is justified, it is justified by faith alone.

But (2) is false. The Bible without question affirms (1) and not its denial. Now, notice that the claim we are making about works is as follows:

> (3) No soul can enter heaven without actual holiness

where "enter heaven" denotes one's ultimate salvation. But is this true from the Bible? It seems clear that it is. The Bible affirms (3), and not its denial:

> (4) A soul can enter heaven without actual holiness.

But notice what is important here: (3) is certainly not incompatible with (1). And since (3) is not incompatible with (1), both statements can be true at the same time; to again use the terminology of propositional logic, they are *consistent* with each other.

But is there some other proposition or line of thought lurking here that might yet reveal these two notions to be contradictory? It appears not. Suppose we were to claim the following, instead of (1):

> (5) A soul can enter heaven with faith alone.

Here we have substituted "can enter heaven" for "justified," and "with" for "by." But (5), according to the Bible, is false. And here we can see just how careful one has to be with these notions. For inevitably questions arise: how can one be justified, and assured of salvation, as the texts mentioned above tell us, and yet still need actual holiness—or, if you will, good works—to enter heaven? Or, to put it another way, how might we say that a soul enters heaven "*by* faith alone," but not "*with* faith alone?" The answer lies in what we have already stated. It is undoubtedly the purpose of God to finally and fully save and secure the souls of all who are justified, but it is also his will to sanctify them before they are finally and fully saved. We can happily agree with a long-standing Christian tradition that it is the work of God by the Holy Spirit within us that produces good works, so that even on occasions where we manifest actual holiness, no one may boast; but we must go further and insist that even these Holy Spirit-produced works are never the grounds of our salvation. The righteousness of God for salvation to all who believe is simply the sacrifice of his perfect Son, and nothing else. But, to state it as straightforwardly as possible, no one enters the presence of the eternally holy God of the universe without *actual* sanctification or holiness. This is, quite simply, what his exalted person demands.

We indeed recognize the difference, then, between being justified and therefore guaranteed of salvation on the one hand, and finally achieving or fully realizing that salvation on the other. The terms "justification" and "salvation," if we mean by the latter term the moment that we are finally and fully rescued and enter heaven, cannot be substituted for each other, for they are not the same event. But, once again, the ground or basis of both events is the same: the person and work of Christ. The New Testament is powerfully clear on this point. Only the practical state or condition of the person involved will be different between the two events, praise be to God; for between his justification and his full and final salvation, the born-again soul will be sanctified. And to this work of sanctification, I should add, we are constantly directed in the Word of God.

Still, Catholics and certain other high-church denominations love to press the issue by appealing to the book of James, which explicitly links the term "justification" to one's works, and to one or two other passages in the teachings of Jesus as found in the gospels, which seem to point to a verdict given on the day of judgment on the basis of works (for example, Matt 12:37, or the so-called parable of the sheep and the goats in Matt 25). This latter point has brought up the possibility of a "final justification" on the basis of works, which has been getting more and more attention in the Evangelical Protestant world. But is it really problematic to hold, as Matthew makes fairly plain, that we will give an account of our lives on the day of judgment, and that God will give us a final declaration regarding our eternal state at that time? And is it problematic likewise to claim that God's final declaration will use our works as evidence of the hidden, inner faith we possess, as Protestants have traditionally claimed of these passages? Troubling as they may appear to some, I see no problem at all with these assertions. Thus, as long as we hold to the clear elements of the gospel, in which we are declared righteous through faith in Christ alone, there is certainly no issue with holding to a doctrine of final justification, as long as it is not said to be ultimately on the basis of works.

Of course, the question remains, to some, whether the view of justification in James truly can be reconciled with the witness in Paul. As Douglas Moo puts it in his commendable, careful commentary, the issue comes down in large part to *when*, according to James, Abraham's justification took place.[5] It indeed requires an act of faith itself to conclude, as Moo does, that James is referring to a future or final justification on the part of God—the text does not clearly lend itself to one interpretation, in my view—but if this is indeed the correct interpretation, then there is no conflict here with the teaching of Jesus or Paul.

THE CALL TO DISCIPLESHIP

But neither of these two practical issues—the popularity of the phrase "gospel-centered," or attempts to reinterpret the gospel by New Perspective advocates—are what this chapter is really about. These two issues, which I have wrestled with a great deal over the years, are important and even essential to reflect on, especially as significant as they have become today; and they are in some sense a necessary foundation for what is to follow. We dare not give up the gospel of faith; neither should we forget the Bible's emphasis on holiness. But there is one remaining issue that I fear has been dangerously neglected; or, when it has been addressed, has often been presented in a manner that is at best unclear or misleading. And it relates to another apparent aspect of the gospel message as found in the teaching of Jesus: his call to follow him in true discipleship.

Again, many books have been written on this particular aspect of Jesus's teaching, and some of them have created quite a stir and even sold many copies. And perhaps no aspect of Christian teaching, including the sovereignty of God over all things, was more emphasized in my own childhood. I can still remember my father preaching on one of the exemplar passages where this call is given, and our small congregation wrestling with the profundity and seriousness of its message. The call had a certain appeal to the poetic among us, including my father and me; it made Christianity appear what it seemed it should be, an all-consuming, all-encompassing thing. One had to die to everything they wanted and everything they were in order to merit heaven; Jesus says it plainly. But as I have grown in my ability to carefully reflect on and think through biblical texts and doctrines, I have returned to these passages again and again to reconsider the validity of the interpretation they were given in my childhood.

The key texts I am referring to are Matthew 10:32–39, Matthew 16: 24–27, Mark 8:34–38, Luke 9:23–27, and Luke 14:25–35. In these

---

5. See Moo, *James*, 135.

well-known passages, Jesus demands that his listeners deny themselves, lose their lives, take up their crosses, and follow him, among other things. In two of the passages, Mark 8 and Luke 9, Jesus's call comes immediately after his announcement that he will be killed; the call in these passages can thus be viewed as a sober warning to those who wish to follow Jesus of what lay ahead, as well as a warning not to abandon him in his hour of need. Thus, it seems, the apparent literal connection between following Jesus and the taking up of one's cross. Furthermore, in these two passages the call is not explicitly universal, or required of everyone. If we limit our interpretation of the call to just this evidence, then, its applicability for today could in a real sense be called into question. We could present it like this: Jesus, like all ancient teachers, had literal followers; there were times when new recruits wanted to join the group; the call to take up one's cross was meant to warn them of the dangers of the enterprise. Just as he warns of the logistical difficulty of following him in other texts (Matt 8:20 and Luke 9:58), so in the texts in question here, he is warning of the physical dangers, and simply asking those who are with him to be faithful when the going gets tough. Under this interpretation, then, the call to take up one's cross and follow Jesus is not an essential element of the gospel message, or necessary for gaining salvation. It is perhaps only for those in Jesus's time, or, more specifically, only for certain people in Jesus's time, those who wanted to follow him more closely. Thus, if we take this line, Jesus's call to follow him may be explained away by either the literal circumstances of his historical time period, or by the notion that Jesus fully intended there to be two levels of his followers: general believers, and those who followed him more closely as full disciples.

But the other passages in which we find this call cast serious doubt on these interpretations. In at least two of the passages, in Matthew 10 and Luke 14, the call to take up one's cross and follow Jesus is set in the middle of extended passages on what it means to be his disciple. In the former passage, Jesus is sending the twelve out on an assignment, and what follows in the chapter is a long set of instructions, most of which is for the twelve disciples directly. But verses 37–39 are best read as part of the message that Jesus wants the twelve to preach to others, and they include the call to love him more than family members, to take up one's cross and follow him, and the warning that to save one's life is to lose it. It seems clear, then, that Christ's call in this passage is meant for all, and is rather serious business. The latter passage, Luke 14:25–35, is worth quoting in full:

> Now large crowds were going along with Him; and He turned and said to them, "If anyone comes to Me, and does not hate his own father and mother and wife and children and brothers and sisters, yes, and even his own life, he cannot be My disciple. Whoever does not carry his own cross and come after Me cannot be My disciple. For which one of you, when he wants to build a tower, does not first sit down and calculate the cost to see if he has enough to complete it? Otherwise, when he has laid a foundation and is not able to finish, all who observe it begin to ridicule him, saying, 'This man began to build and was not able to finish.' Or what king, when he sets out to meet another king in battle, will not first sit down and consider whether he is strong enough with ten thousand men to encounter the one coming against him with twenty thousand? Otherwise, while the other is still far away, he sends a delegation and asks for terms of peace. So then, none of you can be My disciple who does not give up all his own possessions. Therefore, salt is good; but if even salt has become tasteless, with what will it be seasoned? It is useless either for the soil or the manure pile; it is thrown out. He who has ears to hear, let him hear."

Here is one of the most curious passages in all the gospels. Jesus has large crowds actually following him already, and he turns and issues a fascinatingly pessimistic appeal: in order to be his disciple, one must hate their families and even their own lives, carry their crosses, and give up all their possessions. It seems clear, as my father used to say, that Jesus was not interested in large crowds, but in the truly committed. We should note the inextricable connection that Jesus establishes here: following him around in the sacrificial manner he demands is clearly linked to discipleship. And following him in this way requires the complete surrender of every earthly thing, including comfort, convenience, safety and security, possessions, and, of course, one's own aims and plans. It is a total commitment of one's life. Growing up, I was told that this kind of commitment was what was required of me in order to be a true Christian, for to be a Christian and a disciple of Jesus were the same thing. But can this interpretation really be valid? Are we asking too much of these accounts by interpreting them in this way?

We are not. I see no problem arguing that there are elements of the call of Jesus that we see in these texts that are unique to his own time. After all, Jesus is no longer physically on earth; we cannot literally follow him around. One or two of Jesus's demands certainly must be clarified and even mitigated to some degree, in light of our current situation and, I will argue, the evidence of the later New Testament writers in the so-called church age. But the simple truth of the matter is that there is further evidence in these passages, and in other places in the gospels, that makes it clear that the call of Jesus to discipleship is, without question, universal, or for all people in all times and places; furthermore, that this call is inextricably linked to what it means to be a Christian, to salvation itself. And the implications of these truths are incredibly profound, especially for the modern church.

One piece of evidence, sometimes overlooked, is one of the most famous passages in the entire New Testament; it is the passage to which churches have looked for centuries to find the church's mission. It is, quite simply, the Great Commission, recorded in the synoptic gospels. In one account, Matthew 28:19–20, the universality of the call may be clearly inferred: "Go therefore and make disciples of all the nations, baptizing them in the name of the Father and the Son and the Holy Spirit, teaching them to observe all that I commanded you; and lo, I am with you always, even to the end of the age." Here, we are to go and make *disciples* of all nations. This task includes baptizing them and teaching them to follow all that Jesus commanded. Immediately, then, problems arise with the "two-level" view: why would Jesus command his disciples to go and baptize other disciples, if there were, in fact, two levels of his followers, with the more serious category of disciple not being required for heaven? Furthermore, there is a clear interconnectedness here between discipleship, baptism, and following the teachings of Jesus. The inference is clear: Jesus's clear purpose is to make *disciples*, even of the entire world; and disciples are those who become baptized followers of Jesus. Those committed to the two-level view would somehow be forced to conclude that Matthew, for some reason, wanted to emphasize this second level of commitment in his call to the Great Commission, or something similarly problematic. But the clear connection here of discipleship to baptism and the teachings of Jesus, as well as the undeniable momentousness of the occasion, make such a position all but untenable.

In Mark and Luke, though the word "disciple" is not mentioned, the same general duty is commanded: Jesus's disciples are to go into all the world, preach the gospel to every creature, and baptize them. In Mark, a clear connection is made between those who believe and Christian service: *those who believe the gospel message* will do the deeds of Jesus, such as casting out demons, as well as having the ability to do new spiritual works, such as laying hands on the sick. The point here is that even if the term "disciple" is not specifically used, the calling and business of one certainly is. Surely a clear and incredibly profound picture is emerging here: Jesus intends discipleship, which includes accepting all of his teaching and imitating all of his deeds, to be the normal category of believers.

When we pair this evidence with the larger evidence of the gospel of John, the picture is complete. The word "disciple" is used in John roughly as often as Matthew, and considerably more than in Mark and Luke. And in John, we see a fascinating picture. In John 4:1, Jesus is presented as making and baptizing more disciples than John the Baptist. In addition to the link with baptism, which, again, shows that the category of disciple is the norm, it is clear that Jesus was gathering far more actual disciples than perhaps we realize by reading Matthew, Mark, and Luke. In John 6:66, when Jesus's teaching gets serious, we read that a few of his disciples withdraw, and no longer walk around with him. In John 9, in the story of the blind man who is questioned by the Pharisees, the blind man answers their question with a sarcastic retort: "You do not want to become his disciples too, do you?" Their response is likewise instructive: "You are his disciple, but we are disciples of Moses" (John 9:27–28). Again, in these passages, the notion of discipleship seems to be considered the normal category, even to one who was physically unable to follow Jesus around! And there is much more. In John 8, discipleship is explicitly linked with salvation language: after some Jews had believed in Jesus, he warns them with the following: "If you continue in My word, you are truly disciples of Mine." In John 13, discipleship is linked with the distinguishing mark of the Christian message, which is love. In John 15, discipleship is associated with the bearing of fruit, which Jesus proclaims as that which proves that one is a disciple. And on we could go.

And now back to the passages at hand. In Matthew 16: 24–27, Jesus says that those who choose not to follow him are "saving" their lives; but those who save their lives, Jesus says, will actually lose them, when he returns to judge the earth. In a similar passage in Luke 9:23–27, Jesus warns that those who don't follow him will "forfeit themselves." This eternal implication is surely why, in verse 23, Jesus calls us to take up our crosses and follow him "daily." The passages in Mark 8 and Matthew 10 carry this same eternal or ultimate sense. It would be strange indeed, then, if for some people, the "serious" disciples, the call of Christ would have eternal connotations, while for others it would not. The takeaway is clear and unavoidable: in the matter of discipleship, what is at stake is nothing less than eternal life.

WHAT FOLLOWING JESUS MEANS TODAY

To sum up what we have observed here: taking into consideration the larger evidence of the synoptic gospels, the Great Commission, especially as found in Matthew, and the picture of discipleship that we find in John, the view that emerges, as we have said, is that there is really only one category of Christian. The believer in Jesus, without question, must also be a disciple; and the true disciple is one who follows Jesus as he demands. And now we are ready to reconsider the message of our key passages, and face the question at hand, which is simply this: if the call of Christ in these incredibly profound passages is indeed an essential part of the gospel message, and thus clearly meant for all people in all times and places, then how does the call apply to us today?

Perhaps it would be helpful to begin by considering what does not apply today, a far easier task. First of all, as I have mentioned, obviously we are not required literally to follow Jesus around. Neither are we required to be prepared to face the literal and imminent dangers of his arrest, trial, and execution, which are past events. Third, I think it fair to say that there is an element of sacrifice involved in following Jesus in his day that simply does not translate to our own. Think about it: when Jesus warned potential disciples of uncertainties regarding places to sleep (Matt 8:20), he meant it literally. Following Jesus today surely doesn't mean that we are required to sleep outside. Neither does it mean, I contend, that we must abandon all possessions in the radical sense required to follow Jesus literally. Despite the intentions of certain well-meaning authors, then, who seek to unilaterally apply Jesus's demands to the modern world, we must be willing to acknowledge that the difference in circumstances necessitates that we parse these issues a bit more carefully.

So there are aspects of discipleship in Jesus's day that are not repeatable, clearly. But, having already established that the concept of discipleship is the norm for all people at all times, what elements are translatable and repeatable? First of all, very broadly speaking, to be a disciple of Jesus means to learn from him. The very makeup of the Greek word "disciple" relates to learning, or being a learner, as the Bible dictionaries tell us; and perhaps no concept is more closely bound up with discipleship than that of learning. But there is more, obviously; being a disciple of Jesus also means to imitate him. Jesus's disciples weren't mere learners in an academic sense. Jesus had a particular character he both taught and exemplified, and he had a mission, or purpose, in life. His followers, obviously, were meant both to be like him in character and to do what he did. They were recruits, if you will, who were to undergo a time of training and preparation, and were then expected to carry out Jesus's mission. And we indeed see them doing so throughout the gospels and Acts, both during and after Jesus's death. To be a disciple of Jesus, then, means to fully commit to carrying on his teaching, cause, and work. It is imperative that we understand how wholistic the biblical concept of discipleship is.

And this is where the whole discussion begins to take a more serious turn. Clearly, the very concept of discipleship as presented in the gospels requires, as a prerequisite, a robust sense of *devotion* to Christ and his cause. And though it may be that this devotion has a slightly different cast two millennia later in our modern world, the unmistakable essence or core of discipleship that translates to all peoples in all times and places is just this idea of total devotion to the person and cause of Jesus. I believe we can argue with a high degree of confidence that this is what emerges when everything that must be relegated to Jesus's own time and place is removed. I think it undeniable that to be Jesus's disciple today means to have the same level of commitment to Jesus and his cause as those in his day were called to have. In his day, as we have seen, it required literally leaving behind earthly jobs, duties, and even family, to follow him around, and to keep following him around, no matter how hard or dangerous it became. In our day, then, practically speaking, what might this devotion require?

First of all, devotion to Jesus surely requires, at its foundation, *surrender*. Make no mistake: to be devoted to carrying out the mission of Jesus, as devotion to anything might require, involves giving up one's personal interests, pursuits, plans, desires, and ambitions, and taking on those of Christ. I am arguing that this is what the concept of discipleship clearly means to Jesus, but even a scant perusal of the evidence in the gospel accounts reveals that, in fact, Jesus was keen to press this point home. Indeed, apprehending and committing to a radical surrender of self, family, possessions, etc., was something Jesus wanted dealt with *fully and at the outset*. No man could be his disciple, he claimed, unless he had first given up everything, even his own life. Thus, here is the powerful conclusion we must draw from these matters: to be Jesus's disciple demands a comprehensive initial surrender. The notion we have set forth here, that Jesus emphasized these things as a matter of principle, certainly reconciles well with who Jesus was—as the son of God, as is often pointed out, he was no ordinary teacher. Surrendering everything to him, then, must undoubtedly be seen as an act of worship.

If surrender is a necessary aspect of this devotion, so too is *dedication*, its positive counterpart. Though dedication might be thought of as a synonym to devotion, here I mean to emphasize that element of devotion that involves the commitment of one's entire person, including his affections, time, and energy. Surrender, then, can be seen as a *letting go* of something, or leaving it behind; dedication as a *grabbing on* to something, or committing to it. Cleary, no one can be Jesus's disciple without loving him; passages like Matthew 10:37 make the affections a necessary part of this dedication. Furthermore, and quite significantly, one must be completely dedicated to Christ's work; one must leave one's old labor behind and commit to a new purpose, utilizing the best of one's time and energy for this cause. It is worth noting here the urgency or absolute nature of this dedication in the gospel accounts; in one passage, Jesus forbids a would-be disciple even to stay and "bury his father" (Matt 8:21–22), telling him instead to follow him. Clearly, Jesus was in dead earnest that dedication to him and his mission be deep, decisive, and absolute.

Another aspect of this devotion was clearly what we might term *loyalty*. Jesus was serious about his disciples being committed to him no matter what the cost or difficulty, and no matter how circumstances turned out. This notion is clearly seen in the passages that require one to remain with Jesus in his critical hours. Closely tied to this notion is *perseverance*; Jesus wanted to make sure his disciples endured to the end, even during their own persecutions. Matthew mentions this critical requirement twice (Matt 10:22, Matt 24:12–13), and Mark and Luke each once (Mark 13:13, Luke 21:19). What is fascinating and even sobering in these accounts, again, is that only those who endure to the end will be *saved*, as Matthew and Mark put it, or will "gain their souls," as Luke puts it.

This list does not exhaust all that Jesus demanded, of course. This devotion to Jesus includes obedience to all he commanded—an element which, again, marks him as no ordinary teacher. But I list these four aspects of devotion here—surrender, dedication, loyalty, and perseverance—as being those which seem to best parse out what Jesus is getting at in calling souls to discipleship. And so, again, in answer to the question of which of these aspects applies to us, the answer, I believe, is clear: *all of them*. We have already seen that discipleship is the norm for all people in all places. We have also taken into account those aspects of following Jesus that must be relegated to time and place. But, once again, I think it undeniable from the life and teaching of Jesus that discipleship, in essence, involves an all-out devotion to his purpose and cause. If, to be a disciple of Jesus, one must be committed to becoming what Jesus is like, as well as to doing what Jesus did—things that seem inherent in the very notion of discipleship, and which were keenly pressed by Jesus upon all who were interested in following him—then we must hold firmly to all that these principles involve, namely surrender, dedication, loyalty, and perseverance.

One cannot be devoted to the cause of Christ and another cause at the same time; one will have to surrender those other things—even everything—in order to serve Christ as he demands. In addition, one cannot be truly dedicated in time and energy to two different causes. And one cannot waiver in these commitments when the going gets tough, but must indeed remain loyal and steadfast to the end. All of this is what being a disciple, a true follower of Jesus, requires. And to press the point home once again, such devotion is what Jesus requires, and what following him demands, precisely because *this is the kind of devotion to his own calling, and to his own Father, that Jesus himself embodied and lived out*. To be Christ's disciple, then, in the end, simply means to strive to be as much like Christ as possible. And if this is so, and if this indeed is to be the norm for Christ-followers, then the implications for the modern western church are enormous—and, I fear, deeply troubling.

DISCIPLESHIP AND THE GOSPEL

Before we explore further the implications of these things for the modern church, however, there is the matter of the apparent conflict this notion has with the gospel of faith. Suffice it so say, just as repentance must be considered a *sine qua non* of faith, so too must this element of discipleship. There is simply no way to dismiss the demands of Jesus. To do so, again, would force one to try to relegate his teaching entirely to a historical time and place, or to take a "two-levels" approach, or even to postulate a different way of salvation for those who lived after Jesus's time. Some might even be tempted to argue that we must be sensitive to the revelation of redemptive history; just as the truth of Jesus's death and resurrection had not been fully revealed in his own lifetime, so too the full or pure gospel could not be fully expressed until he rose again. But, again, this would be to deny the very nature of who Jesus was, both in his divinity, power, and indeed his knowledge. The teaching of Jesus in the gospels cannot be dismissed because Jesus cannot be dismissed. There may be some progressive revelation in redemptive history, to be sure, but if anything, surely Paul must first be reconciled with his Lord and master Jesus, not the other way around.

In light of these things, then, I am prepared to make the following claim, with all confidence: to the degree that the modern church, or any individual, belittles, downplays, or just plain misses the seriousness of Jesus's call to discipleship, to that degree they have missed an essential element of the gospel message, and of salvation itself. I believe I can go further: to the degree that any individual has failed to apply this ideal of discipleship to his or her own life, or is presently failing to fully accept and strive after this ideal, to that degree their soul is in real spiritual danger. I say this on the authority of Jesus himself, who set forth these demands. One cannot earn one's salvation, to be sure; but one simply cannot come to Jesus, for redemption or any other benefit, without first giving their lives entirely up to him and his service. Jesus inevitably sifted the multitudes, looking for those hearts that were fully surrendered. We dare not miss this essential element of the call of Christ, for to do so is to give up Christ's divine power, authority, and will, as we have said.

I fully realize that in making these statements, I am casting shadows over many of the perspectives and practices of the modern church, particularly in the West. But as Bonhoeffer noted nearly a century ago, this will always be the great temptation of the modern church: to attempt to claim the benefits of Christ's redemption without its costs. But this is precisely *not* what Christianity is about. To utilize the well-known phase, there is no crown without the cross. We will not reign with Christ unless we suffer with him, as Paul himself puts it in Romans 8:17. This suffering results from, inevitably, an all-out dedication to living as Christ in the world, in regard to his character and his mission. And is the church doing this to any real degree in our day? If we look in general at Evangelical Protestantism in the West, it appears not. I believe it is not far off to say that modern Christians, particularly in America, for the most part have no earthly idea what dedication to the person, character, and cause of Christ looks like. Evangelicals are just as dedicated to success, money, pleasure, entertainment, power, and earthly freedom as their secular counterparts. Most of us aren't living for Christ, even superficially so; we are living for ourselves and our own earthly ambitions and pleasures. To say that the western church is genuinely embodying devotion to the mission of Christ is, frankly, absurd. And what I am contending here is that not only is this the root cause of much of our powerlessness in the world, but for many of us, *our very souls are in danger.*

The present western church is almost universally failing to press these demands on its hearers. One must search far and wide to hear anything remotely like this message. And certainly one must search far and wide to see it being lived out. Thank God that in every generation he raises up at least some witnesses to the message of Christ, and we have a few today; but getting the church to respond is akin, as is often said, to turning a giant ship in a hurricane. The great need of the hour, now and always for the modern church, is how to come to grips with the call of Jesus to discipleship, and once again begin to make it an essential element of salvation, just as Jesus did. If the church fails to do this, not only will we be without real power, but again, there is a real question of whether the conversions we are seeing are real. I would like to state the matter again, in the clearest possible terms: I believe that anyone who does not apprehend, carefully consider, and fully commit to following Jesus in true discipleship, understanding that to follow Jesus means to give their lives completely up in service to him, is in danger of missing heaven. As strong and controversial as this sounds, I don't know any other way to read and understand the teachings of Jesus.

If one wishes to protest this claim, appealing, again, to the gospel as presented in later New Testament writers, I would have him once again consider the following: the book of Romans, where the gospel of faith is most clearly presented, actually fully supports this idea of discipleship. Many people stop at Romans 5 in their consideration of Paul's presentation of the gospel. But Paul doesn't stop at Romans 5. His presentation includes chapters 6–8, which insist on the necessity of Spirit-fueled holiness and absolute loyalty to Christ, even in his sufferings (8:17). It is, indeed, those who by the Spirit put to death the deeds of the body who will live (Rom 8:12–17). It is this Spirit, the Spirit who helps us put sin to death, who testifies that we are, in fact, children of God (verse 16)—which seems in direct opposition, I must point out again, to much gospel-centered teaching. Thank God that he will see us through to the end, but the road to heaven, in addition to holiness, also includes tribulation, distress, persecution, famine, nakedness, peril, and sword, all things through which we "overwhelmingly conquer" (verse 37). The point is simple and clear: no one gets to heaven without putting faith in Jesus Christ, but also without following him as a disciple, and joining in his sufferings. Again, some might find it difficult to reconcile these two, but if there is any tension here at all—and I am convinced there is not—it must be maintained.

Throughout the rest of this book, I will seek to explore further the implications of Christ's call to discipleship in various areas of life. For now, the question I wish to press upon us once again is simply this: is the church preaching this message today? Are our "converts" signing up to follow Jesus as he demanded? Or are we preaching the benefits of Christ without the cost? And if we are failing here, what right do we have to claim people as converts? I have been in large churches where the gospel is preached in easy terms to crowds of people eager to make peace with themselves. I am all for preaching a simple gospel, but making converts is easy when the demands are low, especially in the American South, where many are eager to make amends with their culturally-conditioned pasts. But this is not, I fear, true Christianity. Always and forever, Jesus is after disciples, not mere converts; and anyone who fails to consider the full cost is not worthy of him (Luke 14:28–32). There is, indeed, no crown without the cross; and this message is, without question, an essential element of the gospel. May God help his church to recover it; and may each of us, difficult as it may be, examine our own lives afresh, and ask ourselves honestly whether we are truly following Jesus, and whether we are truly on the only path that leads to eternal life—the path that Jesus trod, which goes through the cross.

2

Holiness

My father grew up in the backwater environs of North Louisiana. His father, a World War II veteran who had successfully restarted his life on the GI Bill like so many of his era, worked hard and made a comfortable living in the insurance business. It was the fifties, and for white Americans, I suppose, it truly was a sort of golden age. By the time my dad was in high school his family had moved to a sumptuous house surrounded by lush woods in the suburbs, a structure my grandmother was able to design brick by brick. My father spent each hunting season on an untouched piece of wilderness next to the Tensas River Wildlife Refuge, the last known home of the mythic ivory-bill woodpecker. The Old South was slowly dissolving, but my father was there in its final, (in)glorious heyday. The air was thick in those shadowy hardwood forests, and time was plenteous. Wildlife roamed unabated, and lust and imagination ran unabated, too, though its reaches were bound then, of course, by time and place. He learned to hunt, fish, and track game, all under his father's gifted eye. He learned, too, to love sports, mainly through his mother's influence; she had been Louisiana amateur champion in swimming, tennis, and golf, all at the same time. By the time he hit high school football, his favorite of the four sports he played, he was a lanky six foot three wide receiver with no one to throw him the ball. That all changed with the emergence of his first cousin, Bert Jones, one year behind him but no less precocious athletically. Bert possessed, already, a world-class arm, one that would one day propel him to MVP and near legendary status in the NFL of the seventies.

Their high school coach loved the running game, but it was going nowhere, and with my father's team already five games into his senior season and not doing all that well, it seemed time was running out on my father's potential. Then, midway through the season, the legendary Jones to Hamilton combination was unleashed. The results were spectacular: the duo amassed nearly one thousand yards passing and receiving the rest of that memorable year, which included an unforgettable dual with another Louisiana legend, Joe Ferguson of Woodlawn. At year's end, my father's football talents were obvious, and he was offered football scholarships across the South. There was no question in his mind about which school to choose. LSU had always been his dream, and he had grown up idolizing Billy Cannon and Jerry Stovall. To follow in their footsteps would be glorious indeed.

And follow he did. Throughout his stellar football career, he rewrote the LSU record books, graduating with nearly every major receiving record and strolling around campus like a demigod. Football players were—and still are—idols in the Deep South, and with his best friend Tommy Casanova by his side, and pursued by seemingly every eligible co-ed in the Southeastern Conference, he seemed poised for worldly greatness, outrunning would-be tacklers on mythical Saturday nights in Tiger Stadium while garnering piles of local and even national press. One image, which can be seen in the November 29, 1971 *Sports Illustrated* issue, is burned into my mind: my father, his uniform partially torn away by delirious crowds carrying him on their shoulders, riding that tidal wave of newfound fame and success that never seemed to crest.

Unbeknownst to him at the time, however, there was another movement sweeping the country, one with divine origins. Bill Bright and Campus Crusade for Christ, whatever their ultimate legacy, were going strong in the sixties, leading the aimless youth of the time to meet Jesus. In those days they were earnest and committed, sending missionaries onto college campuses across the country. When one of their fold found my father in his dorm room, the tidal wave of fame had finally crashed. My father found life's meaning and his ultimate purpose upon hearing a clear presentation of the gospel for the very first time. Repenting of his sins and believing in Jesus that very night, my father became a Christian at LSU and never looked back. It was about as sudden and dramatic as a conversion could get.

More success on the football field followed, but so did something else: ministry opportunities. When he was given the chance to speak at the Billy Graham crusade at Tiger Stadium in the fall of 1970, on national television, he accepted. His life changed that day as well. Known to friends and family as a virtually mute introvert, my father couldn't stop talking. The crusade pianist kept trying to play him off the stage, to no avail. When he finally finished and returned to his seat, he began to weep, as Reverend Graham placed his arm about my father's shoulders. The Holy Spirit had loosened my father's tongue and it would never be silent again. Not in the locker rooms of the Kansas City Chiefs and the New Orleans Saints, where he tried to eke out a living in the NFL despite incessant, nagging injuries and a growing discontentment. Not in the classrooms and common areas of Dallas Theological Seminary, or on the city streets of impoverished Dallas neighborhoods, where he honed his skills as a street preacher and evangelist. Not in twenty years of pastoral ministry in the States. And not in the now twenty-plus years of ministry as a church-planter and leadership-trainer in Asia. God's anointing has been on my father in powerful ways.

At least one other thing has followed my father his entire ministry: obscurity. When he finally traded in the cleats for the loafers and finished off his theological training, he was given a ministry opportunity in a small, conservative Baptist town in Louisiana, not far from where he grew up. Preaching a challenging message that stood in direct contrast to the easy-believism of the era, my father's ministry was never fully accepted. His church never had more than fifty members. After a while, no one even knew what had happened to him, so much so that a newspaperman showed up at our door one day to ascertain that very thing. And when my parents finally left America for good, giving up their lives to serve the lost and oppressed of Asia, there was little fanfare and few there to send them off. During his over twenty years of ministry in a large Asian country, he found himself often on remote river ways at night to avoid detection, or sleeping in mud-encased squalor, or squatting over holes in the ground next to snorting pigs. It was as far from the bright lights of western glory, as superficial as that glory may seem to the sentient soul, as one could get. What my father was learning and experiencing, perhaps more starkly than many Christians, is the great contrast between earthly and heavenly greatness, between honor in the world and honor in the kingdom of God. He was following Jesus, and in the process, he was losing his life that he might gain it.

I want to begin this chapter on holiness by considering an aspect of Christ-like character that is perhaps more overlooked or misunderstood than most, but one that is foundational to salvation, holiness, and even usefulness in ministry. I am convinced, again, that the vast majority of Christians in the West really have no idea what giving up one's life to follow Jesus means; but as we saw in the previous chapter, there is a very real sense in which an understanding and coming to grips with this issue in one's own life is an essential requirement of the call of Christ to discipleship. In fact, it could be argued, based on the texts we have examined, that it is *the* essential requirement in this whole matter of following Jesus. And I believe that, after all, there is a very real reason why Jesus's demands to follow him were presented so starkly. For no human instinct, perhaps, beats more strongly in us that than of personal ambition.

AMBITION

If the life of a true disciple—a Christian—is to be marked by a giving up of one's own will and way to follow Jesus, then certain things will follow. In particular, one's *ambition*—defined in the *New Oxford American Dictionary* as "a strong desire to do or to achieve something, typically requiring determination and hard work"—will undergo a radical shift.[1]

The world of secular academia, in particular philosophy and psychology, has long tried to explore and explain the matter of human instincts. One thinks of Freud, who famously tied human behavior to physical pleasure—specifically, sexual desire—and then later, in a curious sort of reversal, sought to establish the "death wish" as a rival instinct. Nietzsche, that other supposed nineteenth-century clairvoyant, famously posited the "will to power" as the basic human urge—something that, in my view, dovetails nicely with Christian teaching on the primacy of love—but, alas, the doctrine remains obscured by scant, vague, and even contradictory explication, a problem that seems endemic to much of continental philosophy. Perhaps, in the end, we don't really need to appeal to the academic world at all. All we need to do is look around.

In the world, ambition is inevitably presented as something good: whatever one has aptitude for, or whatever dream one has, if one works hard enough, they can achieve it. The inherently self-serving nature of this mantra is thus obscured with ostensible virtue; it is one's hard work

---

1. "Ambition," *New Oxford American Dictionary*.

that receives its due reward. We laud such examples and hold them up for imitation. And, in a sense, rightly so, even for Christians; there is strong evidence, particularly in the Old Testament, that a robust work ethic, and even a proper sense of success, honestly achieved, are praise-worthy and even virtuous.

But the coming of our Lord Jesus Christ and the inauguration of his heavenly kingdom stands everything on its head. Indeed, one of the great oversights of many in the modern church, and in particular the Reformed community, I believe, is not only a failure to properly apprehend the radical, transformative nature of Christ's call to discipleship, but also the shift in heavenly focus that takes place with his coming. One thinks, for example, of the Presbyterians, many of whom have exchanged kingdom priorities for earthly ones in the name of redeeming culture; or the so-called Reformed Baptists, whose movement I was part of growing up, who have adopted the Puritan model of the merits of financial success through hard work, but often without taking into account the demands of Christ regarding money and mission. I acknowledge that these are practical outworkings of what certainly can be a complex underlying theological question—the question of how much change and discontinuity Jesus's kingdom and teaching brings, or exactly how the New Covenant relates to all that came before it, but the point needs to be made: the call of Christ to abandon one's life and be devoted to the life and work of Jesus himself clearly and definitively demands that one's ambition—however one defines it, as we will see—be radically reoriented. In discipleship, one takes the focus completely off of one's self and places it on Christ. One's desires, goals, and labor are now given over to learning from Jesus, becoming like Jesus, and doing Jesus's work. In addition, success is now measured by how Jesus measured success—by doing the will of his Father. In fact, the following is perhaps the burning center, so to speak, of discipleship, as it perhaps best expresses the very heart of Christ himself: "not my will, but thine be done." Jesus's entire existence was shaped around imitating his Father and doing his work and will. He had no other purpose for living. And try as we might to explain this away, this radical commitment to the person and work of Christ himself must be, then, the essence of our own discipleship.

The question eventually becomes, of course: what is it, exactly, that Jesus was doing? What was he about? For in answering this question, we will learn our own purpose and mission in life. As tempting as it would be to explore these questions here, however, I want to reserve detailed exploration of these questions for later chapters. For now, suffice it to say, the whole of Jesus's attitude on the matter of ambition can be said to be summed up by our Lord himself in another well-known passage:

> But Jesus called them to Himself and said, "You know that the rulers of the Gentiles lord it over them, and their great men exercise authority over them. It is not this way among you, but whoever wishes to become great among you shall be your servant, and whoever wishes to be first among you shall be your slave; just as the Son of Man did not come to be served, but to serve, and to give His life a ransom for many" (Matt 20: 25–28).

The context of this passage is well-known; the disciples had given in to that basic human temptation to wish themselves great in the eyes of others. In rebuking them, Jesus makes plain both an underlying principle and the scope of his ministry: those considered great in the kingdom will be those who make themselves servants and slaves, which is the purpose of it all—service. What Jesus was doing in his own life, then, was fulfilling the will of God by serving God and others, the only true greatness in God's kingdom. In essence, we become great in God's eyes by giving everything up—in order to make God and others great.

AMBITION IN THE CHURCH

It really is imperative that we hold the mirror up to ourselves and seek to ascertain just how far off the church has gotten in our day. In addition to the sometimes misguided theology of the Reformed community, it never ceases to amaze me how a blatant misapplication of the parable of the talents (Matt 25) still seems to permeate the thinking of many Christians, at least in practice. Whatever "talents" God has given you, the thinking goes, you need to develop and maximize for the glory of God, because he definitely wants to use them in some way. God gives you abilities for a reason. To not develop them is, in the end, sin. Pursue them, develop them, maximize them, and see how much success you can gain from them. Go as far as you can in whatever field you choose; God will use you in that field. Again, even if many Evangelicals don't hold to this principle in fact, they seem to in theory and practice.

The wrongness of this way of thinking should be obvious—but somehow in our day it is not. The call of Jesus to follow him in discipleship cuts right through such thinking with a resounding "No!" Success for disciples is not measured by the realization of our own abilities, but in how fully we live out the will of God—which involves, at the foundation, a complete surrender of self. But there is often a subtle twist in Christian circles: it is viewed as okay to pursue one's talents or ambitions as long as it is for the sake of God's kingdom, or in God's service. But surely this, too, is a mistake. What we have in the church today, it often seems, is a virtual epidemic of people pursuing the development of their own gifts and abilities in the name of Christ and his kingdom. Seminary students pursue graduate degrees to get ahead in their fields. Would-be Christian academics seek publication relentlessly. Those with "artistic" talent record themselves, publish their offerings on the Internet—that enduring temple of self-worship in our culture—and tally the number of views and subscriptions they receive. Outside of the world of ministry, of course, Christians fare no better; life is a competition of promotions, paychecks, and power. In the church and outside of it, then, the situation is clear and acute: Christians seem no different than the world. Very, very few—in fact, it is hard to think of anyone—are truly seeking to give up *all of themselves* to the will of Christ.

Here, then, would be a good time to reemphasize the Lordship of Christ, something that is also inherently part of his call to discipleship. When Jesus called people to follow him, they weren't following an ordinary teacher, of course; they were following someone with the divine authority of God himself. And in Christ's kingdom, he calls the shots, even for those directly involved in specific gospel ministries. John 21:18–22 is instructive on this point: Jesus has just forgiven Peter and given him a divine commission for ministry, but it is Jesus's will that Peter die in a specific way, a way in which Peter would uniquely glorify God. Significantly, Jesus then finishes by telling Peter once again to follow him. In other words, says Jesus, I determine how you will be used, even in ministry; your job is to submit and obey. Peter then asks about John, and Jesus says poignantly: "If I want him to remain until I come, what is that to you? You follow me!" (verse 22). Again, the point is clear: following Jesus means absolute submission to his divine will, which is different for everyone. And just as no one gets to follow Jesus on their own terms, so no one gets to serve him in ministry on their own terms. To follow him is to follow him in everything, for all of life.

How radically different this is from the perspective not just of the world, but of the church today! I will be blunt here: what Christian, or for that matter, what prospective ministry aspirant—or even what current minister—has truly laid everything down on the altar before Jesus and said "not my will, but thine be done?" I recently met a young seminary graduate who wanted to plant a church. Ignoring the needs of the entire world, not to mention other needy American communities, this man planted a church in what was essentially his hometown, not far from where his best friend, another seminary graduate, had also planted a church. The young man informed me of their reasons in person: "I just want to preach, and I want to do it consistently. That's why my friend and I are planting separate churches. We can't both preach all the time." Without judging this man's motives, I couldn't help but wonder: is this what following Jesus looks like? Can it be possible that some are even commandeering the supposed "untouchable" ambition, the "fine" aspiration of the preaching ministry, into the service of their own desires for self-fulfillment? If so, something has obviously gone wrong here.

To be clear, I honestly believe, again, that the church today has a far more serious problem in this area than many realize. If professing Christians are not out living fully for the world, as so many seem to be, then they are pursuing opportunities in the church on their own terms and according to their own wishes. What the church needs desperately is a wholesale recapturing of the radical nature of the surrender Jesus Christ is calling us to. We cannot live for ourselves; we must live for Christ and his mission. And we cannot serve Christ in ministry how we want; he sends us where he wants, when he wants.

AMBITION: THE SOBER TRUTH

But we must go a bit deeper here. Whether Nietzsche meant it this way or not, surely one of the great human urges or instincts is the following, more sinister sense of the word ambition, captured in Merriam Webster's Collegiate Dictionary: "an ardent desire for rank, fame, or power."[2] Christians unequivocally condemn this way of thinking, and rightly so. No one can follow Jesus and seek for these things; such are clearly antithetical to the essence of Christianity. However, I often wonder, frankly, if many Christians are convincing themselves that they are acting for Christ, or out of some sense of "ambition" that in some way is permissible, while in fact they are merely after the same things as the world: rank, fame, and power. Surely any honest person can look inside his or her heart and see

---

2. "Ambition," *Merriam Webster's Collegiate Dictionary*.

the tendency toward these things that we all have. This is, in fact, the temptation the disciples had given into in Matthew 20, quoted above. Thus, surely we must be incredibly careful with any desires we have to utilize our own talents or achieve anything in this life. How easily we can deceive ourselves in this matter!

To be clear, I am not saying here that all senses of the word "ambition" are necessarily sinful; in fact, a theological case can be made, perhaps, for its God-given appropriateness as originally created, and perhaps even for its God-sanctioned purposefulness today. It is, one could argue, a fundamental attribute with which human beings seem to have been made—in particular, some would say, men. This takes us back, perhaps, to our first definition, which refers to a desire to achieve something through our work. It may very well be that God created us, in his image, with a certain apparatus, one that longs for or even by instinct seeks to leave something behind, something one has done; or merely to do meaningful work. And I am not so sure that this is not to some degree even an explanation for the universe itself—the God-motivated ambition of God!

But this is why the coming of Christ and his kingdom is such a momentous event in history. Jesus spoke directly to the "natural," "innocent" things of life, and said that these, too, are to be surrendered to him. Human impulses and instincts, even sinless ones, such as those for work, family, marriage, etc., are to be redirected to God, the blazing center of the universe, and given up if they get in the way. Once again, put very simply, godly ambition is this: giving up one's personal desires for self-fulfillment or greatness in order to make God appear great. In fact, I believe it can be stated in this way: the more of ourselves, our talents, our plans, etc., that we give up for Christ and his mission, the greater we make God look. But again, such surrender and dedication are a basic requirement of being a disciple. Does all this sound too radical? Then I believe we have yet to fully understand what Jesus is calling us to, and what he himself lived out. Zeal for God's house *consumed* him (John 2:17), just as it did David. But who today knows anything of such zeal! What we desperately need is a God-wrought searching of hearts, that Christians in our day may be able to sift through their own ambitions, and see if their desires for self-fulfillment have truly been surrendered to Christ. In the end, of course, only God knows the heart; but we must all carefully examine ourselves. For only then will we know true, Spirit-fueled usefulness for the sake of Christ, that usefulness that comes to one who can truly say "to live is Christ." Again, to be clear, disciples of Jesus surrender *everything* to him—their so-called talents and abilities, their futures, their plans, and their dreams of success. They enter into Jesus's army, so to speak, to be placed where he wants, and to do what he wants. But how many Christians think this way today?

Does Jesus sometimes use our physical talents and abilities for his kingdom? Surely he does, in his own way and timing—and inevitably, I would argue, when we are thoroughly purified of our desires for rank, fame, and power! As Paul puts it in 1 Corinthians 2, usefulness in God's kingdom is not through worldly wisdom or ability, but through the power of the Spirit of God. And the Spirit of God comes, as modern-day hero of the faith Lilias Trotter beautifully testifies, to those who have given themselves wholly up to God:

> Gathered up, focussed lives, intent on one aim—Christ—these are the lives on which God can concentrate blessedness. It is "all for all" by a law as unvarying as any law that governs the material universe . . . Will it not make life narrow, this focussing? In a sense, it will—just as the mountain path grows narrower, for it matters more and more, the higher we go, where we set our feet—but there is always, as it narrows, a wider and wider outlook and purer, clearer air. Narrow as Christ's life was narrow, this is our aim; narrow as regards self-seeking, broad as the love of God to all around. Is there anything to fear in that?
>
> And in the narrowing and focussing, the channel will be prepared for God's power—like the stream hemmed between the rockbeds, that wells up in a spring—like the burning glass that gathers the rays into an intensity that will kindle fire. It is worth while to let God see what He can do with these lives of ours, when "to live is Christ."[3]

Just as it is this very kind of radical sacrifice that is missing in the church today, this radical giving up of one's life, and thus the key to the church's lack of real power, so it is the key to the church's regaining of it. Few people in history have been as talented as Lilias Trotter. As the story goes, she was presented with a unique opportunity to develop her prodigious painting talents, but she gave it all up in service to Christ, and the rest of her life is a powerful testament to the truth of what she describes here. The same could be said of countless other Christians in history, but of course the principle is best exemplified in the life of our Lord Jesus Christ himself, who "emptied himself" (Phil 2:7) so that he might do the will of his Father;

---

3. Trotter, "Focussed," 10–11.

and we see it as well in the Apostle Paul, who willingly suffered the loss of everything so that he might gain Christ (Phil 3:7–8).

In my own life, this principle has been powerfully reinforced time and again. During my first stint on the mission field, my greatest problem was simply my inability to give up my own desires for self-fulfillment and be a nobody for Jesus. I was constantly looking back at what I had left behind, in this case my unfulfilled academic career in philosophy. I was frequently haunting the burgeoning internet chat rooms where other Christian philosophers, many of whom were already in the midst of successful careers, were hashing out new and significant ideas. I longed to contribute my own thoughts to the discussion, and such longing inevitably interrupted my zeal and effectiveness in the ministry I was supposed to be engaged in. Even after later settling down in America with my wife and initiating graduate studies, which appeared absolutely necessary merely to obtain a suitable means of employment, not to mention a legitimate ministry opportunity, the lure of self-fulfillment again drew me in. It wasn't until I had completed my M.A., was enrolled in a Ph.D program, and had begun research on my Ph.D thesis that the providential hand of God drove the principle home for good, persuading me first through outward circumstances and eventually through inward conviction that I should withdraw from the program. First Corinthians 2 became a powerful, watershed passage in my life, and continues to be to this day. Now, I certainly do not wish to apply God's dealings in my own life to everyone's situation, but to my mind the following truth remains clear: God is calling each of us to sacrifice our own desires for self-fulfillment, and even to give up all of our talents and abilities, as significant as some of them may be, for the sake of something infinitely greater—possession by his Holy Spirit, and the supernatural wisdom and power for life and serving others that such brings. Indeed, I do not think such sacrifice is merely for those interested in full-time ministry; I believe this is part and parcel of what it means to be a disciple of Jesus. I am not saying here, of course, that it is always wrong to pursue post-graduate education or anything of that sort. However, I *am* arguing that we need a newfound understanding of both the seriousness and the profundity of what is at stake in this particular issue. In my case, the break has not been easy at times, and in some sense the pangs and the longing are still there, made more acute by the realization that I could have made at least some genuine contribution to philosophical problems that are at least to some degree meaningful. But the principle remains: God's desire for each of us is that we demonstrate his worthiness by first giving up our own talents and opportunities for fulfillment, so that his will may be preeminent and his power may be displayed in and through us. And as many pastors and theologians have pointed out, if he gives certain opportunities or pursuits back to us, that is his business; ours is first to give them up to follow Christ.

As Lilias Trotter puts it in the quote above, the spiritual law that governs God's universe is simple. The more of ourselves we give up to God, the more of his power he unleashes in our lives. "Narrow as regards self-seeking, broad as the love of God to all around." This is true Christian ambition. May God help us to regain it! Imagine for a moment what would happen if all professing Christians today truly and fully surrendered their lives to the will and service of Christ. The Holy Spirit would be unleashed in real power; the world would no doubt be transformed.

COVETOUSNESS

I will attempt to speak more to this issue of surrender, especially as it relates to ministry, in a later chapter. For now, when considering this issue of holiness, especially as it relates to Christ's call to discipleship, it is only fitting to consider, next, the issue of covetousness. This is obviously not the book to dive into this issue in any detail, but since comfort, leisure, and wealth are so abundant in our own time and place, and since our Lord spoke so often and so clearly about it, surely a few comments are in order.

In the interest of biblical fidelity, again, it is imperative that we are sensitive to the historical and literal circumstances that gave rise to Jesus's rather radical-sounding calls on this issue, including the aforementioned Luke 14:33, in which Jesus plainly tells a crowd of would-be disciples that in order to follow him they would have to give up all their possessions. It is surely likely that this was meant literally; Jesus was looking for those who would follow him immediately and without reserve. And following him around clearly meant that one must literally give up all their possessions, at least in some sense. Surely, then, this command does not translate to our modern world?

To answer this question, other, abundant evidence is at hand, in the form of Jesus's general teachings on the issue of money and material possessions. In the well-known Sermon on the Mount passage, in Matthew 6:19–21, we are told not to store up treasures on earth, but treasures in heaven; for wherever our treasure stores are, there our hearts will be also. In other words, whatever we amass or stockpile indicates where our hearts are. In the parallel passage in Luke 12:33, we are told to sell our possessions and give to charity, in order to make for ourselves unfailing treasures in heaven. In Matthew 6, Jesus adds to the treasure passage by commanding us not to worry about even our necessities; we should instead trust God to provide our needs. For, Jesus tells us, the Gentiles eagerly seek all of these earthly necessities; we are instead to seek first God's kingdom and righteousness, and all these things will be added to us.

Of course, Jesus had much more to say about money and material possessions throughout the gospels; a notable passage earlier in Luke 12 instructs us to "Beware, and be on your guard against every form of greed" (verse 15). To try and sum the matter up, it is clear from the teaching of our Lord that he was greatly interested in his followers showing both their love to God and their trust in him by (1) a genuine disregard for earthly wealth, and (2) a sincere and deep trust in God for the provision of their needs.

Practical writers on this topic often complicate matters unnecessarily, perhaps; but before we attempt to analyze the matter any further, it would perhaps be useful to briefly examine what the rest of the New Testament witness has to say on the matter. A classic passage in 1 Timothy 6:9–12 warns in strong language against desiring riches, exhorting the man of God to be content with food and covering, to "flee" love of money, and to pursue godly character and spiritual warfare, clearly echoing the teaching of Jesus. Oddly, when many discuss this issue informally, it has been my experience that the later 1 Timothy 6:17–19 is a favorite passage used by some to seek to "balance out" this earlier passage or the strong teaching of Jesus. However, the clear emphasis of Jesus's teaching on money speaks to the *desire* and *pursuit* of money, which Paul himself clearly forbids in 9–12. Thus, while it is possible for one to gain and possess riches in the normal course of one's work, the exhortation in 17–19 to those who are rich clearly echoes the teachings of Jesus, in telling them to "store up for themselves the treasure of a good foundation for the future, so that they may take hold of that which is life indeed." The mention of "life indeed" emphasizes the magnitude of what is at stake in the matter of covetousness, just as Jesus presented it.

The New Testament's teaching on money, then, is clear and unified. But what about the witness of the Old Testament? Here, suffice it to say, there is general agreement with the New Testament; but there can be no doubt, in my mind, that Jesus is upping the spiritual ante, so to speak, in the inauguration of his heavenly kingdom. Once again, though it is certainly beyond the scope of this book to explore the matter in detail, surely one can easily see the intensity and single-minded focus of Jesus's call to discipleship and his teaching on such matters as money. In light of the clarity and force of Jesus's teaching, then, as well as the divine authority which he definitively claims, I have no problem asserting that the teaching of Jesus on money is not only normative for believers, but as such is noticeably stronger than the teaching of the Old Testament on the matter.[4] Having grown up in the Reformed community, I can say that it is rather astonishing the lengths to which some theologians will go to reconcile Jesus's teaching with the witness of the Old Testament. But the resulting stance, in my view, inevitably fails to do justice to what the New Testament is calling us to. Jesus's teaching on money and possessions constitutes, again, a powerful shift, one that undeniably reflects the arrival of the kingdom of heaven.

The question that remains, then, is simply this: how are we as modern Christians, especially in the West, failing in this critical area of discipleship? A brief reflection surely informs us all that we are not doing very well. I can personally attest to the fact that after returning from a third-world country to the United States, it truly is remarkable how complex and expensive life in the West can be, especially during times of difficulty, such as the ongoing COVID pandemic. Still, it is likewise remarkable how easily one can slip back into a lifestyle of comfort, entertainment, and security! The money we westerners, particularly in America, spend on unnecessary pleasures, worthless and often sinful entertainment, and security, for our own futures or our children's, is truly baffling to consider. Again, there is no need for a "guilt-trip" here, but there is also no room to attempt to get around the clear teaching of our Lord Jesus and his call to radical kingdom-oriented living. Simply put, we are to live more and more for heaven, using more and more of our resources for those heavenly purses which will not wear out. We are to undertake liberal generosity for those in need, in Christ's kingdom and beyond. And we are not to desire or pursue greater and greater riches, and, as some modern writers

---

4. I have become wary of attempts to find a unifying principle that represents the teaching of both testaments on this issue. For example, the bulk of the New Testament evidence strongly (and, I would argue, uniquely) emphasizes *sacrifice, sharing,* and *equality,* and not, say, *stewardship* or some related notion, which is often put forward as a unifying principle.

have pointed out, luxuries. Such is completely unwarranted in the life of a follower of Christ. And yet professing Christians all over America seem to ignore the clear teaching of Christ on this matter.

Few practical areas of the Christian life are as sensitive as this one. Conversations between Christian brothers and sisters on the issue inevitably turn tense. And it is not just defenses of one's "liberties" that provoke conflict; surely it is evidence of how out-of-touch Americans are on this issue that political discussion inevitably dissolves into fears of "socialism" and the loss of economic freedom! I will discuss political issues directly in a later chapter, but I can't help but mention it in passing now, especially as such fears apparently are growing exponentially in the current political climate. What it comes down to for many American Christians, it seems, is simply an unwillingness to compromise certain elements of their lifestyles, which they are increasingly rationalizing. Again, I have felt the dangers acutely in my own experience since returning to the States; the temptation to upgrade one's comforts and conveniences remains something about which one must maintain the utmost vigilance.

Admittedly, it is sometimes difficult to go beyond these rather general principles and discuss specifics. Consider a single mundane example: cars are necessary entities in many western countries. One perhaps may justifiably purchase a certain car on the basis of its long-term value, or simply on the rationalization that cheaper cars cost more to maintain in the long run. Who is to say where the line between a wise investment and an unnecessary luxury is to be drawn? Perhaps, in the end, the wisest approach on such matters is to return again to the issue of helping those in need. The New Testament in general places an enormous emphasis on sharing and giving, first to those of the people of God; 2 Corinthians 8:1–15 may be seen as paradigmatic of this point. Here, Paul indicates that those in the body of Christ who have "an abundance" should supply those in the body who are in need, so that there may be an "equality." That this is a policy for the church, and not necessarily the State, is obvious; but where are the western Christians who are taking this seriously? The physical needs of the larger world, including the larger Christian world, are staggering. How in the world can we western Christians justify our excessive lifestyles, with its unnecessary comforts and expenditures? The time is ripe for eternal investments; for helping those in need in the name of Jesus, and for funding gospel endeavors in his name. The church must rise up, shake itself awake, and begin to take this matter seriously. Hard stances must be taken; lines must be drawn. In short, we must repent of our covetousness and outright selfishness.

Perhaps a final warning is in order; it behooves us to recall that Jesus's demands regarding discipleship are, in the end, *required*. Our divine Lord who calls us to discipleship also utters these sober words, recorded in all three synoptic gospels: "It is easier for a camel to go through the eye of a needle, than for a rich man to enter the kingdom of God." And elsewhere: "Woe to you who are rich, for you are receiving your comfort in full" (Luke 6:24). And in the tragic destiny of the rich man, as told in Luke 12:16–21: "So is the man who stores up treasure for himself, and is not rich toward God." God takes this matter seriously because it is so near to our hearts. Make no mistake: God wants to be our treasure, and no man can serve two masters (Matt 6:24). Once again, these are matters of eternal significance.

IMMORALITY

There is another problem endemic in the church today, and it is sexual immorality. Though this issue doesn't relate as ostensibly in the gospel accounts, perhaps, to Christ's call to discipleship, it certainly relates directly to the denial of self, which Christ clearly called us to in following him; and in this whole matter of holiness, especially in our ungodly day and age, we would do well to reconsider this issue with all seriousness. It is certainly an area of sin I and every male friend I have ever had have battled—mostly, though certainly not exclusively, in our youths. And as an older pastor recently conveyed to me, as if he was discovering the dangers and temptations of our modern world for the first time: with inventions like the Internet, it is remarkable that any normal American man can remain blameless in this area! There can be no doubt that the church has been in some sense nearly destroyed by problems here; may God help us carefully to consider exactly where the problems lie, and where help may be found.

One should begin by acknowledging that from the standpoint of Christian morality, our culture has been in an undeniable decline. Moral declines, if one has had the privilege of studying history, are well documented in societies that have been blessed with economic prosperity and a measure of freedom. One thinks of Rome, for example; as historian Livy puts it in the preface to Book 1 of his magisterial classic *The History of Rome*:

> To the following considerations, I wish every one seriously and earnestly to attend; by what kind of men, and by what sort of conduct, in peace and war, the empire has been both acquired and extended: then, as discipline gradually declined, let him follow in his thoughts the structure of ancient morals, at first, as it were, leaning aside, then sinking farther and farther, then beginning to fall precipitate, until he arrives at the present times, when our vices have attained to such a height of enormity, that we can no longer endure either the burden of them, or the sharpness of the necessary remedies. This is the great advantage to be derived from the study of history; indeed the only one which can make it answer any profitable and salutary purpose: for, being abundantly furnished with clear and distinct examples of every kind of conduct, we may select for ourselves, and for the state to which we belong, such as are worthy of imitation; and, carefully noting such, as being dishonourable in their principles, are equally so in their effects, learn to avoid them. Now, either partiality to the subject of my intended work misleads me, or there never was any state either greater, or of purer morals, or richer in good examples, than this of Rome; nor was there ever any city into which avarice and luxury made their entrance so late, or where poverty and frugality were so highly and so long held in honour; men contracting their desires in proportion to the narrowness of their circumstances. Of late years, indeed, opulence has introduced a greediness for gain, and the boundless variety of dissolute pleasures has created, in many, a passion for ruining themselves, and all around them.[5]

To Livy, then, Rome's moral decline, which he characterizes as an increase in greed and a love for pleasure brought on by growing wealth, is something all should learn from. In our own culture this decline is easily marked. If there is one virtually indisputable sign of it (at least from a Christian point of view), it is that of what we might call *public acceptance*. It used to be, for example, that society demanded that a woman be dressed decently and with modesty in public. Today female nudity is more publicly tolerated and even celebrated in the West than in any other developed nation in history. We are now at the point, after the "Metoo" movement, which rightly drew attention to the predatory activity of certain men in positions of power, where women are being encouraged to dress as provocatively as they wish. And this is to say nothing of the publicizing of sex, which has obviously reached perverted levels. The fact that

---

5. Livy, *History*, Preface.

pornography has been interpreted as having constitutional protection in America for a half-century now, and that the easily accessible Internet displays every sexual perversion the human mind can conceive at the click of a button, is almost impossible to fathom.

I say all this not to make any other point—although much can be drawn from this, to be sure—than that we Christians need to be aware of the waters we swim in, the air we breathe. This ain't our daddy's world, to be sure. To be frank, it ain't even ours anymore. In adolescence, my lusty friends and I would roam the barren roadsides desperate for a discarded magazine with even a glint of sun-faded nudity in it. Our standards were low, in more ways than one. Thank heaven we didn't have the Internet. If we did, there is no telling where we would have ended up.

There are, no doubt, multiple causes for the immorality epidemic that has taken over even the church. Livy, perhaps, said it best; the more leisure we have and the more pleasure we experience, the more we seek, unless God has mercy upon us. And the more we obtain, the more twisted our desires become, of course. It's the way our brains work, as we all know; the more we experience of a certain pleasure, especially in the realm of sex, the less stimulated by it we become; new and strange allurements are needed. It's no wonder our culture is so perverse; we've been at this for a long time now. But for the church, it's a deadly serious matter. Sin is the quickest way to lose the Holy Spirit and bring on God's discipline.

I think we need to start where Jesus started. Jesus preached holiness as essential to entering heaven, let us remind ourselves; the gate is small and the way narrow that leads to eternal life, and there are few who find it (Matt 7:14). Also, Jesus, as we all know, was interested in purity getting all the way down to the heart (Matt 5:27–28). And his solution for sexual temptation is as stark as it is simple: "If your right eye makes you stumble, tear it out and throw it from you; for it is better for you to lose one of the parts of your body, than for your whole body to be thrown into hell. If your right hand makes you stumble, cut it off and throw it from you; for it is better for you to lose one of the parts of your body, than for your whole body to go into hell" (Matt 5: 29–30).

This is serious stuff. One could argue for hours about the degree to which Jesus's words here are hyperbolic, but I think the safest way to state it is that Jesus is simply emphasizing the utter seriousness of sin, holiness, and judgment. God is not playing games with sin; if it remains unrepented of, one's ultimate destiny is clear. So, what are we to do? The first step is to agree with Jesus about the seriousness of sexual sin. It is tempting at times to think the church has failed to handle aspects of this problem with any degree of balance. An example: some Evangelical churches have allowed ministers who have fallen into actual fornication or adultery back into the pulpit, at times with frightening rapidity. Surely this shows complete ignorance of the seriousness of holiness as presented in the New Testament. A contrasting example: pornography is often looked upon, especially in Southern Baptist circles, in a sort of fundamentalist way akin to alcohol and (in a bygone era, anyway) dancing; if you touch it, you're tainted, sometimes for good. Pornography seems to have a stigma attached to it, which smacks of fundamentalism. I am convinced that immoral thoughts, especially if indulged in and utilized for self-gratification, can be just as displeasing in the sight of God as glances at pornography. And yet, pornography is inevitably seen as "an extra step," presumably as it brings in some added element of sin, though what the nature of that added element is in this perverted world, where women's bodies are provocatively displayed everywhere one turns, is hard to say.

We needn't let this devolve into a philosophical discussion on the nature of sexual sin, of course; alas, as meaningful philosophical discussion is clearly beyond the level of most Southern Baptists, such would be pointless. Nevertheless, I have seen countless ministry job applications where the subject is asked whether he or she has viewed pornography, and if so, how recently; but what is the point of depending on such questioning if the subject's heart is not in the right place? If immorality is plaguing his or her mind and thoughts? If he or she is consistently lusting after other people's bodies in everyday life? If he or she is emotionally unfaithful to their spouse at the workplace? And on we could go. The point here is that we can talk about degrees of sin all day long, but when it comes to the New Testament, there is a sense in which it's all the same to Jesus. It's a pure mind and heart he is interested in; anything less is unacceptable.

Sex between a loving man and woman in a committed marriage relationship is as holy and sacred to God as anything on earth, and we must hold it in the highest esteem. But I think it helpful for our purposes here to focus not on the obvious sinfulness of various violations of marriage, but on the very acute and unique dangers of it. And here I do wish to focus on pornography. Humans have lusted over, fantasized about, and violated sacred bonds with each other since the dawn of time, but there can be no question about the incredibly dangerous and seductive nature of photography and film, especially since the invention of the

Internet. It is remarkable indeed that these relatively recent inventions have facilitated so much human sin and perversion, and are now being used by Satan to keep the church, including many ministers, hopelessly mired in discouragement and spiritual uselessness. As if the human heart needed any more grease on its rails! So many strategies have been offered to combat this problem; I myself have profited much from reflection on fantasy's complete disconnect with reality. It is warped and diseased indeed to go constantly chasing after mirages and shadows. Pornography presents a chimera: sex, female behavior, etc., are clearly *not* the way they are so often presented in its perverse, male-dominated world. But before we examine how to combat this sin, we should turn our attention to a remarkable fact about human nature, one which should absolutely transform how we think about our struggles with sin.

UNDERSTANDING HUMAN NATURE

I believe strongly, and I believe the Bible bears this plainly out, that human beings, whatever their remarkably unique powers, in whatever way they are distinct from animals, and whatever their souls consist of—all things that are notoriously difficult to meaningfully comment upon—are, in a very important and even foundational sense, *physical* creatures, creatures moved, and even controlled by, physical passions and desires. Now, I would love to unpack and defend these notions in detail, but obviously such rather philosophical inquiry is beyond the scope of this book. And I don't wish to go too far here, and make claims that are, frankly, beyond where even philosophy and science have taken us on these issues, but I will assert that as controversial as these claims are, they are not without strong defense in the history of philosophy at least. Certainly they are in science as well; science is keen to present man as a creature of basic physical desires, similar to animals, of course, in being merely the apex of animal evolution; science has long been committed to naturalism, and we all know where that leads. But one need not be committed to methodological naturalism, or be a materialist, I contend, to agree with what I am claiming here. In philosophy, this notion was perhaps most memorably put forward by the great philosopher David Hume, in his landmark *A Treatise of Human Nature*, where he famously contends that "Reason is, and ought only to be the slave of the passions, and can never pretend to any other office than to serve and obey them."[6] Hume's basic but very powerful contention here is that reason, whatever it is or does, is under the full control of the *passions*, or our emotions, feelings, and desires;[7] when there is a supposed change in reason, it is because there was first a change in passion, and the only thing that can oppose or overturn one passion is another, stronger passion. Of course, such musings are part of controversies that go all the way back to ancient times, and are explored by various Christian authors such as Jonathan Edwards, who, it seems, had views that at least approach those of Hume.[8] But the question that matters here, of course, is what the Bible says.

I contend that Hume's view, despite his well-known aversion to religion, does have remarkable echo in the Bible. Several key passages are of particular interest. One is the critical moment in the garden of Gethsemane where Jesus informs his disciples that "The spirit is willing, but the flesh is weak" (Matt 26:41). His meaning seems obvious: no matter what we know we should do in our minds (spirits), there is another power, what he calls our flesh, that can overcome whatever we know we should do, or, better put, our desires to do what we know we should. This seems to coincide with Hume: the problem, to put it crudely, is not in our *thinking*, but in our *feelings*. Our passions overcome our reason; the flesh inevitably wins out. Jesus then drives the point home: the solution is to have a higher power, a higher energy, motivating us. We must "watch and pray" that we might not enter into temptation. Only God's power will do. Again, this echoes Hume: only a greater passion within us can produce change.

Paul echoes Christ's teaching in the famous passage in Romans 7: there are two powers at work within us. They are not reason and passion, as is popularly asserted; they are, quite simply, flesh and spirit. We are, Paul contends, creatures of the flesh. There are many times when we know the right thing to do in our minds, but we cannot do it. We must have the prevailing strength of the other power: the Holy Spirit. Only His help will do. And this teaching is powerfully attested to in such other

---

6. Hume, *Treatise*, Book Two, Part Three, Section Three.

7. This interpretation of Hume's term "passions" is provided by Rachel Cohon in her article on Hume's moral philosophy in the *Stanford Encyclopedia of Philosophy*. See Cohon, "Hume's Moral Philosophy," §2.

8. I would argue that Edwards, both in *Freedom of the Will* and *Religious Affections*, argues for a similar influence of the passions on human action, though in the latter work he is more interested in the relationship between body and soul, for obvious theological reasons, and not passion and reason, like Hume.

passages as Galatians 5:16 and following, where we are told that the only way to defeat the flesh is to "walk by the Spirit."

The biblical picture of human beings that emerges, then, seems very close to what Hume, of all people, was arguing. And whenever atheistic philosophers agree with the Word of God, perhaps we had better pay special attention! Note that I am certainly not arguing that in Hume a clear, uncontroversial, or definitive theory of human nature emerges; far from it. Nor am I arguing that the Bible itself clarifies all the complexities of the human mind, will, and soul. Again, far from it. For sure, if one wishes to avoid out-and-out materialism, and posit the existence of the human soul, a notion that certainly has New Testament support and that goes back to the early days of post-apostolic theology, these matters are complex indeed. However, I contend that the Bible does make clear two very, very important realities, which we must never forget if we wish to win the battle against sin: 1) we are creatures of *flesh*, whatever that entails, and 2) the only hope of overcoming, controlling, or guiding our flesh is the Spirit of God. I continue to believe strongly that identifying "flesh" with our emotions, passions, and desires, is the best way to make sense of the biblical data; I believe as well that it is important that we understand our emotions, passions, and desires as essentially physical entities. At the very least, however, we must be persuaded of one and two; especially two.

Gaining and maintaining God's power, then, is of critical importance in our fight against sin. We will touch on this more in the next chapter. But before we move on, we must return to the words of Jesus. I believe a tremendous amount of good could be done if Christians would only take his words in Matthew 5:27–28 more seriously. For the simple truth of the matter is that there are many times when we are not walking in the Spirit. Furthermore, sin, like many crimes, is opportunistic; when the availability presents itself, it will strike, often without warning. And it is indeed remarkable how strong temptation is when *possibility* is increased! The connection is obvious, to be sure, but speaks to the very problem Jesus is addressing. There are times and situations where sin is, for all intents and purposes, inevitable. There are right eyes that simply *will* cause us to stumble, no matter what we do. The treatment Jesus offers is undeniably effective: get rid of your eye.

I am aware of the need for holiness to be a heart issue—Jesus himself speaks to it—but here our Lord is simply being practical, and I think we must adopt a similar approach. If, for example, a particular scenario inevitably results in my sin, I have to remove the possibility of the scenario itself. It's as simple as that. If I have a problem with alcohol, and being alone with alcohol inevitably results in my drinking it, then I cannot be left alone with alcohol. If having unmonitored Internet access tempts me to search for inappropriate images, even if on occasion, I simply cannot have unmonitored Internet access. It really is this simple. However, it is remarkable how few Christians are willing to make the necessary sacrifices to avoid sin! The ultimate cause of sin, to be sure, is our lack of the Holy Spirit—this is a truth we must maintain—but why in the world would we allow a potential instrument of serious sin like the Internet to ever pass unfiltered before our eyes? When so many inappropriate images can pop up even by accident? The world is simply too full of sin for Christians to be in any sense relaxed. I have no hesitation in saying strongly that I believe no Christian, especially, frankly, no male Christian of any age, should have unfiltered or unmonitored use of the Internet, or, honestly, of any video device. One cannot be too careful. The only question is: who is willing to pluck out right eyes or cut off right hands? What, in the end, are we willing to do?

Again, there is no question that what Jesus wants of us, to be sure, is a heart-felt, Spirit-filled love for him that is so great, so powerful, and so passionate, that our sinful desires are overwhelmed and overcome by his grace within us. But to be so full of the Spirit all the time is simply not reality. We are to seek this, strive for this, and be satisfied with nothing less than this, to be sure. And we must strive for holiness above all. No one should be content with anything less than blamelessness, although perfection certainly will not be attainable in this life. No one, minister and ordinary Christian alike, should tolerate obvious sin like pornography to any degree, or lusting after others that we see in person, or inappropriate thoughts, or any other sin. I would point us, again, to the teaching of our Lord: we cannot let sin keep us from the kingdom! It must be defeated! But sin cannot be defeated without real sacrifice on our part. We will talk later about knowing more of God's power in our lives, but for now, what are we willing to do to be holy? What sacrifices are we willing to make? And if we hold back, what does that say about our souls? Services must be disconnected, access filtered and monitored, and private time properly managed. *Now.* Our very souls are at stake.

LOVE

The issue of love is surely the appropriate one to end on in this discussion on holiness. We are examining Jesus's call to discipleship, and we are highlighting key areas of holiness that are closely bound up with that call. And as we have seen, love is one of these; for no one can come to Jesus unless they love him supremely. Beyond this, however, love to God and man is presented by Jesus as the greatest of all Old Testament commandments; indeed, everything else in the law and prophets depends upon it (Matt 22:34–40). And Paul presents love in the later New Testament as the crowning jewel of all Christian virtues (1 Cor 13). Clearly, then, any discussion of Jesus's call to discipleship, and Christian ethics in general, must center on the virtue of love.

A great deal has been written on this topic in the past thirty or so years, much of it from the pen of authors such as John Piper; and it would be appropriate to acknowledge as well these authors' debt to eminent theologian Jonathan Edwards and his classic *Religious Affections*. Piper's work in particular has been subject to sufficient criticism by various pundits, mostly on Internet blogs; whether or not it has all been warranted is another matter. Suffice it to say here, one should always be wary, as we said previously, of slogans, catch-phrases, and movements gathered around supposedly novel ideas; surely the Word of God should be considered sufficient to guide and instruct. But to the extent that Piper's work has been genuinely explicative of the Word of God, to that degree, I believe, it has been profitable.

There should be no doubt whatsoever that God intends the affections to be of primary or foundational importance. This is surely what loving God with one's heart truly means. And if we examine the original context of the first and greatest commandment, a strong case can be made for the affections:

> "Hear, O Israel! The Lord is our God, the Lord is one! You shall love the Lord your God with all your heart and with all your soul and with all your might. These words, which I am commanding you today, shall be on your heart. You shall teach them diligently to your sons and shall talk of them when you sit in your house and when you walk by the way and when you lie down and when you rise up. You shall bind them as a sign on your hand and they shall be as frontals on your forehead. You shall write them on the doorposts of your house and on your gates. Then it shall come about when the Lord your God brings

you into the land which He swore to your fathers, Abraham, Isaac and Jacob, to give you, great and splendid cities which you did not build, and houses full of all good things which you did not fill, and hewn cisterns which you did not dig, vineyards and olive trees which you did not plant, and you eat and are satisfied, then watch yourself, that you do not forget the Lord who brought you from the land of Egypt, out of the house of slavery" (Deut 6:4–12).

It is remarkable that even in this Old Testament context we are told to love the Lord our God, with everything within us. Notice that the word "love" here is the operative term; the command is to *love* God. But God seems already to have anticipated the tendency of human beings to manifest incomplete expressions of love; thus, the added elements of "heart," "soul," and "might." Whatever one thinks about the full significance of these terms here, it seems clear that our love to God must be heartfelt (the affections) but also extend to obedience.

But I think Edwards's special emphasis on the affections finds support here: verse six repeats our Lord's desire that his commands be on our *hearts*. And I believe the subsequent directive, that we should surround ourselves with all God's commands, speaks also to the issue of the affections. So, too, does the warning that we not allow other things to so take our affections—when we "eat and are satisfied"—so that we no longer care for God. This passage, along with the language of delight to be found scattered throughout the Bible, in particular in the Psalms, also makes Piper's emphasis on delight tenable, if a bit overemphasized. I say nothing about his emphasis on the personal pursuit of joy, and his system of so-called Christian Hedonism; it is surely clear from the Word of God that our duty to love God is overwhelmingly "God-centered." There is no doubt, as Edwards pointed out throughout his works, that God intends the happiness of his creatures, but their happiness is to be derived from fellowship with God. They seek God because they love God, and they seek God because they know it pleases Him. It has been stated sufficiently, and I concur, that to the degree that Christian works such as Piper's focus on pursuing *joy*, and not on pursuing *God*, to that degree they must be rejected. But again, to delight in God, or to give him our first and complete affections, joy, satisfaction, etc.—all of which, to be sure, are terms that involve, necessarily, the emotions—is the basic duty of the Christian. And those who seek to do so *will* be utterly and eternally satisfied in the fullness of who God is, though such fullness is ultimately inexhaustible.

Thus, undeniably, all souls are commanded to have a delight in God and his things that we must seek to cultivate above all other delights. More than this, however, this delight is meant to be *absolute*. The command to love God comprehensively is surely brought to full fruition in the New Testament, where Jesus demands a love to him that overwhelms all other loves, as we have seen in our Lord's call to discipleship. One could certainly argue that this all-consuming delight and devotion to Jesus extends beyond his person to his purpose and also his people; but the exclusivity and singleness, if you will, of the love that Jesus demands in his call to discipleship is impossible to miss. And, so, we can safely say that delight in the person, work, deeds, mission, and kingdom of Jesus should be foundational. And how desperately we must fight to maintain this affection in the world in which we live!

But there is a profound warning about the delusional nature of emotional delight in the teachings of Jesus, who speaks repeatedly in John of the necessary connection between love and obedience. Loving Jesus also means keeping his commandments. The emotions are by nature fleeting and transitory. In fact, if one wished to make serious claims about the nature of love, especially within theological discourse, surely a careful examination of the matter—utilizing, perhaps, a rigorous study of human nature—would no doubt be incredibly helpful. A problem Jesus knew as well as any was that despite its foundational nature, human passion is subject to fluctuation, regression, distraction, and, as we have seen, subjugation by other passions. The disciples illustrated this better than many; thus Jesus exhorts them after his resurrection to obedience. It would also be an interesting study to seek to ascertain the precise way in which delights and affections become deeply rooted and settled in the human mind; many of us can happily admit that despite a lack of outward, demonstrable joy in God on occasion, there remains a quiet burning, a deep resolve to continue to honor him, esteem him, obey him, and live for him, that can only be described as genuine love. The affections or passions are still there, though perhaps not always to the same felt degree; yet somehow they seem more deeply rooted.[9]

Regardless, the most coherent and perhaps even the most biblically-faithful way to leave the matter is to make the following related claims, much in agreement with Edwards, Piper, *et cetera*: (1) having affections for or delight in God is essential to pleasing him; (2) having affections for

---

9. Hume seems to be referring to such experiences when he speaks of the "calm passions"; see again Book Two, Part Three, Section Three.

or delight in God is the only proper foundation of God-pleasing obedience—in other words, without it, there is no true obedience; (3) having affections for or delight in God *inevitably leads* to obedience, provided this affection is carefully cultivated and deeply felt; and finally, (4) such deep affection and its attendant obedience can only be produced in us by the Spirit of God. This last point we will return to later. We can thus sum up the matter in this simple way: the love that Christ demands involves a genuine affection that is deep enough to produce real, long-lasting obedience to all that he asks us to do. And let us not forget—the first thing he asks us to do is to maintain and cultivate affection for him!

So what are we to say about the modern church? The application is obvious. There are so many things vying for our affection today that Jesus, His words, and His kingdom often have little room in our hearts. There are basic pleasures like food, drink, romance, sex, fun, and entertainment that compete with and often overwhelm our love for God; but there is also the above-mentioned lure of self-fulfillment or power. All of these earthly loves are rampant and endemic in our culture, and, sadly, in the church as well. If we were completely honest, we would have to admit that many times there is very little interest and delight at all in God's things in our souls, or at least it isn't very deep or absolute. At best such delight is confined to narrow portions of our day or week. Very few of us know anything of making the will of God our very "food," as Jesus put it in John 4:34. The results of this lack of delight in God are predictable: many of our daily affections, passions, and pursuits have nothing to do with the mission of Jesus. We even work hard to rationalize our pursuits as those of Christ, even though we know, deep down, that they are fundamentally self-serving. We will talk more about the mission of Christ later—about what the church is to be doing—but the main point to emphasize here is that whatever Jesus was doing, he was doing with all of his affection. This brings me to the last thing I feel compelled to mention in this section: there is an aspect or expression of Christ's love that I believe most fully and deeply represents the ultimate example of love to God on earth; and it is *zeal*.

The disciples recalled, it is said in John 2:17, that it was written of Jesus that "zeal for Your house will consume me." Delight in God—being satisfied in him—and even obedience to God are not, perhaps, the Scripture's ultimate statement on the matter of love, it could be argued.

Zeal, as Leonard Ravenhill puts it, is "love ablaze."[10] Notice that the Old Testament words spoken of Jesus are in the context of him cleansing the temple. Zeal, then, is when our delight in God so overflows, that we are overcome with a burning desire to see him honored and glorified in the world. And when God is not thus honored and glorified, as is so pervasively the case in our world, that zeal consumes us, as seems to be the meaning of the term both in its original context, Psalm 69, and in John 2. It may even be argued, as many theologians have pointed out, that Christian zeal—this all-consuming passion for the glory of God—is the foundational motivation of the entire universe![11] Delight is the foundation, the source, of love, to be sure; but zeal is its full expression. And notice the contrast with perhaps that most basic, or at least insidious, of human motivations: human ambition, a desire for self-fulfillment or power. The call to discipleship beckons us instead to the great heartbeat of God himself, and it is indeed the foundational human duty—the call to live, breathe, and burn for God himself, and not for ourselves. Zeal for God, then, empties us of all thoughts of self. It engulfs and consumes our very being, so that nothing of self-interest is left. We pursue the glory of God at all costs, or no matter what may become of us. We should note in passing here as well that it is this utter selflessness that forms the basis of that other aspect of love, which is love to man. It is only true selflessness that can fulfill the great calling of 1 Corinthians 13. It has indeed been well said that the opposite of love in the Bible is, in fact, self. And we should point out that even if all is ultimately in some sense self-serving, as philosophy and science have sometimes told us, then our ultimate picture remains unaltered: love is getting pleasure solely from the happiness of God and other people.

If what we have said of zeal is true to any degree, then the modern church is in dire straits indeed. But if we are to be like Christ, then we must pursue this zeal: this delight in God that consumes us. It will produce an all-out, passionate determination that will stop at nothing to see God's name and will honored, obeyed, and carried out in one's life, in the

---

10. Ravenhill, "Zeal," https://www.lastdaysministries.org/Groups/1000087727/Last_Days_Ministries/Articles/By_Leonard_Ravenhill/Zeal_Love_Ablaze/Zeal_Love_Ablaze.aspx.

11. I leave as homework for the reader the matter of reconciling this assertion with our earlier speculation that perhaps the God-motivated ambition of God caused him to create the world. It is fair to say, however, that the idea that God's zeal for his own glory is foundational to creation has a long history in Christian theology, most notably in the work of Edwards.

church, and in the world. This passion will undoubtedly take up the lion's share of our energy, labor, and time. It will become our one all-consuming desire. Nothing on earth, not even the legitimate, wholesome pursuits of life, will ultimately be able to distract it. And though it might run in bursts and spurts, it will continue, and, ideally, build and grow, until at the last we are transformed into those burning, shining lamps the Bible speaks of (John 5:35)—those that make a real difference in the world, no matter what the cost. But how faint and dim our souls often flicker in this dark and needy world! It is indeed true that to have this zeal we need to be continually refilled and reignited by the Spirit of God. And for this, we need real holiness, real sacrifice—and real prayer. And so, to this most essential—and neglected—aspect of the Christian life we now turn.

3

Prayer and the Holy Spirit

I'LL NEVER FORGET THAT morning. It had been a typical Sunday service in the enormous but generally solid church my family had recently joined. Sure, the music was superficial, obnoxious, and downright sensual at times—it was a Southern Baptist church, after all—but the messages contained some truth and the people seemed sincere, and now the next step in our involvement lay before us. Having been pushed—if not lovingly browbeaten—into volunteering in some way, and despite the fact that almost all of our available time was taken up with various odd duties, prayer, and concern for our previous missionary endeavor, which was ongoing in Asia, my wife and I decided to go ahead and take the step of getting more involved. For me, the choice was simple: I was going to join the prayer team. And though my wife certainly had a heart for prayer, she decided to help out in the children's ministry, since the church desperately needed volunteers in that area.

As I walked out the sanctuary doors toward the prayer room, I was hopeful. The church did not speak of prayer often from the pulpit at the time, but they were proud of this particular prayer meeting. Taking a cue from the ministry of Charles Spurgeon, church leaders had decided to have prayer take place during every service. The sole point of the meeting, we had been informed, was to pray for sinners to be saved as the gospel was being preached. I was generally encouraged by the obvious trust in God, and despite the fact that the pastor was about as far from

Charles Spurgeon as one could imagine, I was hopeful of finding something meaningful to be a part of. I had been raised to consider prayer the most foundational of all activities in the Christian life. I had been part of all-night prayer meetings and frequent times of fasting and prayer, and I had known real men and women of prayer in my time. My father had even prayed with Leonard Ravenhill. And despite the fact that, to be sure, I undoubtedly lagged considerably behind these giants of prayer in my own prayer life, I still had aspirations of achieving more consistency and power. God *had* helped my wife and me to pray over the years, without question—but we were always aiming for more. And if this church was really serious about intercessory prayer, then we would be on to something.

They weren't. What clued me in first on the way to the prayer room was the buffet line. A lavish breakfast spread, clearly intended for volunteer workers, lay before the entrance to the prayer room like a celebratory gauntlet. Since someone was watching, I felt obligated; the donuts, snacks, fruit, coffee—was that eggs and bacon?—couldn't go to waste, could they? This was church money, for heaven's sake. I was new to the whole mega-church thing, but I couldn't help but wonder whether the Metropolitan Tabernacle had a spread like this for its volunteers. Somehow, I doubted it; but then, I couldn't imagine Spurgeon's church having a nursery full of screaming children, either. Was the food incentive or reward? Did we need it just to make it through the next half-hour? It was hard to guess what the thinking was here, but when I finally finished nibbling on a cinnamon roll and headed off to the prayer room, I was starting to get a bad feeling. When I entered, my fears were confirmed. It was disappointingly small. And completely empty.

Something wasn't right. This was a massive church, numbering thousands upon thousands of members. And this was the main service at the main campus, which was always packed to the gills. *Where was everybody?* I wondered. I sat down in one of the plush chairs and waited. After what seemed like a considerable amount of time—I was worried that the sermon was about to commence—an older lady walked in, followed by another. One was quite old; the other, I was to shortly learn, was from a third-world country. It was a beautiful picture of the body of Christ, to be sure, but about as far from being representative of that particular church as you could imagine, which was right then full of young, slick, middle-to-upper-middle class white couples raising their hands and swaying to their favorite worship ditties.

After some short introductions, we began to pray. I was thrilled to hear both ladies pray with sincerity and real fervor, even though one of them consistently fondled a string of what looked like prayer beads and made unintelligible gurgling noises when she wasn't praying—probably not representative of the majority of the church either, I wagered. No one else entered the prayer meeting that day, nor any Sunday for a period of weeks. Over the months that followed, at times one or two young seminary students drifted in, but often they didn't pray at all, and they almost never came back.

After some period of time, a new campus was launched near our hometown—the main campus was forty-five minutes away from our house—and after a while, we decided to attend there and join its prayer team. One Sunday I found a sign and a small circle of chairs, and I waited. Finally, a man peeked his head around the door; it turned out he was the leader of the prayer team. Why he wasn't praying I didn't know, but it turned out he knew my father, and he eventually shared that he wanted to move on from leading the prayer team. After a period of time in that campus, I volunteered and was allowed to lead it.

Nothing changed. One faithful brother and I prayed together for the better part of a year, but no one else joined in for more than a Sunday or two. Even the pastors, who were instructed by the main campus church leadership to be part of a new campaign to get more prayer in the campuses—thank God for that, at least—never stayed and prayed more than once. It was borderline bizarre. Most days, I went at it alone during the two worship services. I eventually expanded the prayer meeting to include other requests, did some advertising, and tried to stay faithful, though the devil quieted my voice on occasion as well. But I felt it was doomed from the beginning. The same reality I had seen all over the world my entire life, and the same reality I was still trying to fight in my own life, was abundantly evident here: prayer is not something most Christians engage in with any degree of real seriousness. It's simply too hard and too personally unrewarding. And when new prayer endeavors are undertaken, the devil moves swiftly and powerfully to snuff them out. I have known for some time now that this is a tremendous, gaping problem in the church today, one that not only puts the church in extreme danger, but one that tells us much about the state of Christianity in general. Because prayer, the Bible tells us, is the one thing we must do, with all of our hearts. All the time.

THE DIFFICULTY OF PRAYER

It would be foolish to attempt to defend ourselves on the matter of prayer, surely. The Bible calls us to prayer repeatedly. And anyone familiar with the Bible at all should not need to rehearse the full range of verses on the topic, especially in the New Testament, starting with the teaching and example of Jesus, and featuring prominently in the letters of the Apostle Paul. It is thus undeniable that prayer is an indispensable and even critical aspect of following Jesus, and as we have said, it is absolutely vital in this whole matter of gaining the spiritual power we need to do so.

What stands out in many New Testament passages is the bothersome notion of *time*. Jesus tells the disciples a parable in Luke 18 so that they would pray "at all times" and not lose heart. Paul says the same thing in many passages; we are to pray "without ceasing" (1 Thess 5:17), to "devote" ourselves to prayer (Col 4:2), and to pray "at all times" (Eph 6:18). Again, throughout the Bible, and particularly in the New Testament, prayer is incredibly prominent, even central; and it is nearly always presented as something that needs to be done *continuously*.

We as modern Christians are so far from this it is almost laughable. Churches no longer have prayer meetings, or if they do, they are exceedingly rare, or mixed with Bible studies or praise times, and all but eclipsed. Small groups, ideal opportunities for focused prayer, often share the same fate. Private prayer, for many of us if we were honest, is inevitably swallowed up by the business of life, entertainment, or some other thing, and never fails to fall by the wayside. The result is that prayerlessness has become a distinguishing mark of the modern western church. Of course, there are many such marks, but the main problem with prayerlessness, as we shall see, is that the Bible presents it as absolutely foundational to spiritual vitality and usefulness.

It may be that some Christians are genuinely untaught on the importance of prayer, but this seems unlikely. I believe the prayerlessness of the church comes down quite simply to the failure of church leaders to emphasize it. There were those in the past who were "men of prayer," though the reality of the Bible is that every Christian should be known as a person of prayer.[1] But the fact that our ministers and church leaders

---

1. The designation of certain people as "prayer warriors," a phrase utilized quite a bit in Evangelical circles, is itself a sign of the woefulness of the times; according to the Bible, of course, all Christians are to be prayer warriors. There is simply no other way to live the Christian life. Some may be particularly gifted in prayer, to be sure, but no

today speak so little of it, and lead by example so poorly in it, exacerbates the problem. Regardless, the truth is, I believe, that all of us know how important prayer is; the problem is in the doing of it.

Let me attempt to be more specific, and utterly straightforward, about why Christians today don't pray. First of all, prayer is hard simply because it requires Christians to be engrossed in things that are not detectable by the senses. When one prays, one has to close one's eyes and attempt to imagine that God is real; then one attempts to speak to this invisible God. It is not so much that we lack faith, though we often do; the problem is simply the practical difficulty of concentration and imagination. Are we too dependent on our senses in the modern world to pray? If not, then we are certainly too over-stimulated to sit still for very long. The second problem with prayer is that it takes time, silence, and solitude, things that modern people are increasingly unable to tolerate in our lives. We can blame the moving image, the slow-down of time due to modern conveniences, and other things all we want; this still won't excuse us in the sight of God. But the third and main thing that keeps Christians from prayer is one we all know about: prayer requires a unique and focused interest in spiritual things. By interest I mean delight in, affection for, zeal concerning, etc.; all the things we spoke of in the previous chapter, where we discussed love for God and his things as an aspect of discipleship. I have suggested a model for human nature that coincides at least to some degree, I believe, with the Word of God. In that model, human passions, or our emotions, feelings, and desires, lead or produce our actions. If this is the case, then we don't pray simply because we don't want to pray, or because we are not moved to pray. Surely this is largely uncontroversial; whatever we think the relationship between human emotion and action is, it is obvious that we often don't do certain things because we have no interest in doing them or because we want to do other things more. And prayer, sadly, is consistently moved down the list of things we want to do, it seems.

Note too, here, that we often *do* pray, with great passion and energy, when we are strongly moved in our emotions; usually this occurs when someone we love is hurting, or in times of personal crisis. There exists, then, at least some clear evidence of the relationship between the passions and prayer. One of the great tasks of the Christian, then, is surely to cultivate a passion for those things that we should be praying for all the time, as the Bible implores us to.

Christian is to be outdone in terms of time and energy given to prayer.

WHY WE MUST PRAY

But first: why pray? And why is it that the Bible implores us to pray "at all times?" The answer from the Bible is easy to find, but incredibly difficult, apparently, for many Christians fully to comprehend or accept. And it is here that the Bible's presentation of human nature comes fully into view. As we have already said, the Bible makes it clear in many, many places that *God's strength*, through the agency of his Spirit, is the Christian's only hope for holiness. Not only that, but God has intended it that way from the beginning. "Not by might nor by power, but by My Spirit, says the Lord of hosts" (Zech 4:6). Though it is most evident in the New Testament age, when the Holy Spirit has been uniquely sent into the world, it is clear from the beginning that God wishes to be our source of all good, of spiritual strength. For it is this that gives him glory. It was *his* might that rescued the nation of Israel, and through miraculous works of *his* power, brought them out of Egypt. It was his strength—through the medium of intercessory prayer, symbolized through the raising of hands—that gave Israel the victory against Amalek in Exodus 17. And on and on we could go, of course. The very essence of prayer, in fact, is just this: an appeal to almighty God for help, either for ourselves or others. Of course, prayer is also the means by which we worship God, thank God, etc., but no other sense of the word comes through in the Bible like this. It is quite simple: we can't please God in the flesh (Rom 8:8). We have no strength of our own to do spiritual good. Our only hope is the power of the Holy Spirit poured out in our souls. And God designed it this way, so that he could get the glory and honor. And this is to say nothing of the spiritual enemies we face, or of the difficulties of life, which we can do nothing about. In all of this, God alone can help us.

The picture of prayer that we get from saints in the Bible, then, is one of careful *dependence*. Men and women in the Word of God prayed to him with consistency and urgency because, first and foremost, they truly needed him. "But I, O Lord, have cried out to you for help, and in the morning my prayer comes before you" says David in Psalm 88:13. Indeed, throughout the Psalms we see God's people crying out to him repeatedly, often in the early morning or even throughout the night. The dependence of the Son of God himself upon his Father in prayer, well documented in the gospels, is a beautiful picture of the necessity of consistent prayer. And as Jesus himself taught us, the relationship between prayer and obtaining the help of God's Spirit is clear: "how much more will your heavenly Father give the Holy Spirit to those who ask him?" (Luke 11:13). It is no wonder, then, that Paul exhorts us to pray at all times. Those who know the truth about themselves, who have understood or experienced their own weaknesses and failures, who know the absolute necessity of the power of God, are people of prayer. And those who don't apprehend these things, it would seem, are simply untaught from the Scriptures.

HUMAN NATURE REVISITED

We began discussing human nature and our need of God's Spirit in the last chapter, but perhaps it would benefit us to go a bit deeper into this topic, and to relate it specifically to the matter of prayer. For in my experience in different churches here in the States and around the world, it seems that people have a vague understanding and agreement of what we have said so far about prayer, but because these issues are often not explored in detail from our pulpits, education in these things is inevitably shallow or of little consequence. And then there is the messy problem of God's sovereignty, which discussion of prayer inevitably leads to. I don't want to dive too deeply into these turbulent waters here, but if there is one reason at least to recommend a serious study of Reformed doctrine, it is on this very point. Indeed, there is so much confusion on this matter in the church today that it is hard to know where to start.

Suffice it to say, a large number of professing Christians today seem convinced that we possess free will, and are able to take "the first step," at least, toward pleasing God by accepting him in faith. They are convinced that people must choose God on their own, and that they have the power to do so. It is astonishing, really, how pastors and churches have allowed this sort of thinking to creep back into the church, because it is—as, thankfully, several Christian thinkers have recently pointed out—nothing short of heresy. It is simply Pelagianism or semi-Pelagianism reworking itself back into the church,[2] which was fully condemned at the Second Council of Orange in 529 C.E., as any good encyclopedia will tell you.[3] As philosopher Kevin Timpe—himself a proponent of free will—puts it,

---

2. See, for example, Baker, "Why Christians," 463, where she argues that such views are "commonly endorsed in sermons and other forms of popular Christianity."

3. See, for example, *Encyclopedia Britannica*, "Semi-Pelagianism," https://www.britannica.com/topic/semi-Pelagianism.

the position of the church, at least since Augustine, has always been that "No human individual in the *status corruptionis* is able to cause or will any good, including the will of her coming to saving faith, apart from a unique grace."[4] Simply stated, no human being can do any good apart from God's power. I pray that the Evangelical church will come to a newfound awareness of the superficiality of its doctrine of salvation! But what I am arguing here, in essence, is that the necessary connection between spiritual good and God's power *before* salvation is not nearly as prominent in the Scriptures as the necessary connection *after*! Such passages as Romans 8 and Galatians 5 make it absolutely certain that no one can do any spiritual good at all in the power of the flesh. That is why Paul's division of the two categories of flesh and Spirit is so critical for Christians to understand. But we have an incredible aversion in our day, it seems, to God's sovereignty, and to serious study of the Bible in general. People long ago stopped believing in the necessity of their utter dependence on God. Perhaps this is why prayer, too, has fallen by the wayside.

Of course, just plain distraction by the world, and interest in other things, is undoubtedly the foundational cause of our prayerlessness. But the point here should be clear: if we absolutely and utterly need the Spirit of God in order to please him at all, then we must seek it. And we seek it primarily through prayer. In fact, the Bible speaks of the Holy Spirit assisting us to pray (Rom 8:26), and it also tells us of a unique reality, a sort of pinnacle of Christian usefulness: of prayer "in the Spirit" (Eph 6:18, Jude 20). Clearly, then, the Holy Spirit and prayer have a unique relationship, one that we had better learn more about, and seek earnestly to experience. And if the Holy Spirit is helping us to pray at some times, then it becomes clear just how urgently God the Father wants us to pray. Think about it: the Holy Spirit Himself, the third person of the Trinity, is praying to the Father with "groanings too deep for words" (Rom 8:26). As mysterious as this is to consider, it is even more humbling and even frightening. No wonder that Paul, through the agency of the Holy Spirit in the inspired Word of God, speaks of prayer so often and so seriously. Again, it is, apparently, a great work—perhaps, in some sense, *the* great work—that Christians are to be about.

What is emerging, then, is a picture like this: God, the great creator of the universe, is working in us and in the world for his good pleasure (Phil 2:13), according to his own will (Dan 4:35). One of his great aims

---

4. Timpe, *Free Will*, 57.

is to redeem and purify a people for his own possession (Titus 2:14), that we may do good works and proclaim his excellencies in the world (1 Pet 2:9). The power by which all of this is accomplished is the Spirit of God himself, poured out into the souls of men, as we have seen. Thus, in order to be obedient to the will of God and seek to accomplish his purpose for us, we are to seek his power in our lives, which is not automatic, but which must be constantly and persistently sought, through the agency of prayer. This picture becomes especially acute when we understand the nature of the other enemies we have, including our own flesh, which battles against the Spirit (Gal 5:17), but especially the devil and all his followers (Eph 6:12–20), against whom we are utterly helpless without God's strength, and who are constantly seeking those they may devour (1 Pet 5:8). We must therefore "keep watching and praying" (Matt 26:41), lest Satan sift us like wheat (Luke 22:31). We must, indeed, "keep alert" in prayer, being "devoted" to it, praying also for others and for the work of God in general (Col 4:2–4). Clearly this is deadly serious business. Few Scripture truths are as clear as this: we are in way over our heads in our battle against sin and Satan. Only God's power will do, as only God's power has always done; but oh, how the church today is failing to apprehend these things! Our lack of seriousness in prayer is, indeed, one of the great failures of the modern church.

Now, some might interject by pointing out a problem: if we need God's help for everything, then we need God's help to pray as well. In other words, how can we be blamed for our prayerlessness, when we first need God's help to do it? My response is to acknowledge that this is indeed a legitimate philosophical problem, and one that gets right to the larger problem of God's sovereignty and man's responsibility, things I worked on extensively in my graduate studies. Such matters are certainly worth exploring, but we do not have the space to work them out in any detail here. For now, we must let the matter stand where Scripture has it, by acknowledging these two truths: we are absolutely dependent on God's power, his Spirit, for any good work, and we are also responsible for obtaining that power. There are many things we could say to attempt to reconcile these two, of course, but what I am emphasizing here is that many Christians do not seem to be aware of, or willing to accept, the first of these truths, while the second, though problematic, is clear in Scripture. At the very least, one thing we should add to our prayer list is the request that God help us to pray!

HOW WE SHOULD PRAY

Practically speaking, then, how shall Christians begin to honor God more in this crucial matter of prayer?[5] First of all, I believe a "legalistic" approach is unhelpful. The Bible contains too many references to daily prayer to dismiss it, of course, but I have found that Christians far too easily begin to think of such daily efforts as duties. There is a sense in which they are duties, to be sure; we have a duty to worship God, and certainly our need to seek him daily is something he deserves. But, again, I have found that the one time I get up and attempt to seek him and fail at it, the sense of guilt that follows is unhelpful. Perhaps it is best if we begin to think of daily "devotional" times as practically as possible. The principle is simple, and goes along with what we have been saying: if we don't seek God earnestly every day—ideally, it seems, before the day begins—or at least as consistently as possible, we are setting ourselves up for failure. Going back to the heart is essential here, as always. When we don't seek God, we need to ask why. Many times, of course, we are simply too tired, too sick, or simply too busy to have meaningful times with God every morning. And this is why many Christians have designated prayer in the afternoon or evening as their time of more intensified prayer, especially intercession for others.

Anyone raised in church has surely heard this word "intercession"; it is actually closely bound up with the Hebrew word for prayer, and involves someone intervening on another's behalf. It is toward intercession for others, then, that all Christians must incessantly strive. To be an effective intercessor, though, requires several critical elements. First of all, it requires holiness; it is the prayer of the righteous man that accomplishes much, we are told in James 5:16. *Purity* in prayer is something that many don't consider, but if one has time to work it out, it is considered an essential element of effective prayer in the Scriptures. Thus, I believe the first thing we must do to become more effective intercessors is to focus on our own holiness. In Psalm 15:1-2, David tells the Lord that he who would abide in his tent, and "dwell on Your holy hill"—that is, he who would draw near to God, and have intimate communion with Him—must be one who "walks with integrity, and works righteousness." In Psalm 24:3-5, David tells us again that only one who has "clean hands and a pure heart," who has not involved himself with sin, can "ascend into the hill of

---

5. Some of what follows was first published in my little book *Prayer: The Church's Great Need*, and appears here with the permission of Grace and Truth Books.

the Lord," and "stand in His holy place." Proverbs 15:8 says that the prayer of the *upright* is God's delight. Isaiah says in chapter 33:14–16 that only one who "walks righteously and speaks with sincerity" can dwell with our Lord, the "consuming fire." First Timothy 2:8 tell us that we are to lift "*holy* hands, without wrath and dissension." First Peter 3:7, in addressing specifically the husband/wife relationship, exhorts husbands to live with their wives in an understanding way, so that their prayers "will not be hindered." Clearly, holiness is necessary for effective praying.

Another thing we should aim for is *persistence*, or perseverance. We are to keep asking, keep seeking, and keep knocking, we are told in Matthew 7:7, and our request will be given to us. Paul tells us in Ephesians 6 to "pray at all times." In Romans 12:12 he tells us to be "devoted" to prayer. And in I Thessalonians 5:17 he tells us to "pray without ceasing." This is certainly the kind of prayer Paul himself was doing; in chapter 3:10 he tells them he is praying "night and day" that he may be able to see them.

And we are to pray *passionately*. James 5:17 tells us that Elijah prayed *earnestly*. "*Beseech*" the Lord for laborers to be sent into the harvest, our Lord Jesus tells us in Matthew 9. Paul tells the Thessalonians in I Thessalonians 3:10 that he "night and day" keeps praying "*most earnestly*" that he might see them. "With *all my heart* I have sought you" says the psalmist in Psalm 119:10; indeed, they are blessed who seek him in this way (verse 2). In Acts 12, the people of God sought him with *fervent* prayer that he might let Peter escape from prison. And Paul tells the Colossians in Colossians 4:12 that Epaphras is "always *laboring earnestly* for you in his prayers."

Intercession, in the end, is what the majority of the prayers in the Bible essentially are. But many of us never get past the platitudes of habitual prayer and into this real heart of biblical praying. Our Lord's model prayer, after all, was simply that: a model, or outline, if you will. In the Old Testament, there is a vivid picture of intercession in virtually every book; the intercessory prayers of Moses, David, Solomon, Ezra, and Daniel form some of the great prayers of the Bible, and are eminently worthy of study. In the New Testament, the church age, we find intercession even more prominently displayed. Our Lord Jesus commanded us in Matthew 9:38 to "beseech the Lord of the harvest to send out workers into His harvest." In Acts 4:29, we see the church of God crying out to the Lord to "grant that Your bond-servants may speak Your word with all confidence." The apostle Paul says of the Jews in Romans 10:1 that his "heart's desire" and "prayer to God" was for their salvation. In Ephesians 6, Paul pleads with the people of God to pray for all the saints, and also "on my behalf, that utterance may be given to me in the opening of my mouth, to make known with boldness the mystery of the gospel . . . that in proclaiming it I may speak boldly, as I ought to speak." And in Colossians 4:3–4 he asks for prayer that he might make the gospel "clear in the way I ought to speak." Indeed, the success of every aspect of a gospel endeavor depends upon God; thus Paul in the same passage pleads for the Colossians to pray "for us as well, that God will open up to us a door for the word, so that we may speak forth the mystery of Christ." In 2 Thessalonians 3:1 he asks for prayer that "the word of the Lord will spread rapidly and be glorified." In Acts 12:5, we see that fervent prayer was being made for Peter, who had been put in prison. Paul exhorts us in I Timothy 2:1ff to pray for all in authority, so that Christians "may lead a tranquil and quiet life." In Ephesians 6:18 he exhorts us to pray for "all the saints"; and we are told in Hebrews 13:3 to "remember the prisoners."

Now, how in the world are we to begin to meet this immense need for intercession? Who of us can hope to rise to the level of some of the great prayers and praying saints in the Word of God? The only hope, first, is to return to prayer for *ourselves*. No soul can achieve real purity, real persistence, and real passion in prayer for others unless that soul is itself aflame with the Holy Spirit's power. The apostle Paul tells us that his own prayer for the Ephesians was that God "may give to you a spirit of wisdom and of revelation in the knowledge of Him . . . that the eyes of your heart may be enlightened, so that you will know . . ." and he goes on to list several wonderful spiritual truths that he is praying the Ephesians would truly understand, and that would become powerful, encouraging realities in their own walks with God (Eph 1:15ff). Thus even a proper understanding of God and his Word, and certainly a deeper, more spiritual awareness of heavenly realities, are given to us by God in response to prayer. Paul lists a similar prayer in Colossians 1:9ff. In this prayer, his main desire is that we would be able to "walk in a manner worthy of the Lord, to please Him in all respects." Our only hope not only for right understanding, but also to live according to God's Word, in true holiness, is the power of God, which comes through prayer. And as we have already mentioned, the apostle explains clearly in Ephesians 6 that prayer is a major weapon in our fight against the devil and his "spiritual forces of wickedness in the heavenly places." And, of course, our Lord had already told us this in Mark 9:29, and in his model prayer as well, where he tells us to pray to God to "deliver us from the evil one." Thus we are to pray constantly for God's deliverance from temptation and from the devil and all his schemes, which are arrayed against us.

Surely we are beginning now to see the absolute necessity of prayer, both in our own lives and for others. The Bible exemplifies and exhorts us to prayer on virtually every page. What emerges, again, is that prayer is the great work to which we must surely strive to be dedicated. Again, it is first of all for our own hearts. If grace and sanctification depend in large measure on this real, spiritual power that we have been discussing, and if this power—even to understand, believe, and get grace from the Scriptures—comes uniquely through the means of prayer, then our responsibility is clear. And if we are called to this matter of consistent intercession for others as our chief work, then we had better set about making time for prayer. If we fail on a morning to do it, we must pause and get alone with God in the afternoon. If we go a few days without interceding for those in need—a failure in love, to be sure—then we must quickly remedy the problem. And if we can't pray alone for very long, due to fatigue or distraction, then we need to find someone to pray with! I am not convinced of the inherent spirituality or necessity of long prayer times, unless one has a great many people to pray for—which perhaps we should—for Jesus himself warned against long prayers. The model prayer, indeed, is almost shocking in its concision, and virtually every prayer we have recorded in the Bible is similarly brief. What I am convinced of, instead, is intensity. Surely it is better to spend ten minutes of intense prayer to God than twenty minutes of mostly daydreaming. Or thirty minutes of serious prayer—which would be genuinely taxing, if the prayer was truly intense and if one was actually praying the whole time—than the fabled "sweet hour." The last thing the church needs is to grow defeated or discouraged by an undue consideration of the issue of time. We don't need popcorn praying or sentence prayers, to be sure, unless the situation demands it—but we don't need protracted prayers either, especially if they are passionless. Or in a public prayer meeting. What we need is continual effort at it. To pray at all times, I believe, means to keep coming back to it; to pray repeatedly.

I believe the church's calling is clear. Regardless of small doctrinal differences, the church, even Christians from different churches, need to get together to pray. Groups of two, four, ten, thirty; in person, before, during, or after services, even on video chat—the people of God need to pray. But this is often the last thing one finds in churches or conferences.

It is truly frightening how neglected prayer is. People will travel hundreds of miles to hear others preach, as my father was fond of saying; but no one wants to pray. The reason, again, is clear; prayer is difficult and personally unrewarding, especially private prayer. But the fact of the matter is simple: once again, it all comes down to our hearts. We simply must begin earnestly to seek after the same heart for prayer that we find exemplified in the Word of God. Not necessarily for its own sake, of course, but for the sake of all the things people in the Bible were praying for. We must align our hearts with God's interests, and pray those interests back to him. If what we have said is true, then a clear and unmistakable sign of the Holy Spirit of God in a person's life is fervent, persistent prayer. Let's not miss it: if God is interested in his own will and glory being displayed in the world, and if the Holy Spirit is that agent on earth who is passionately pursuing it, even praying for it, then the soul that looks most like God is the one who, fueled by the Spirit, is passionately pursuing God's glory in prayer. It really is that simple. And if Christians are *not* pursuing God's will and glory in Spirit-fueled prayer, then what can we say about them?

THE HOLY SPIRIT RECONSIDERED

I have said that the church has failed to rightly apprehend its need of the Spirit; indeed, in the end, a failure to think properly about the third person of the Trinity is perhaps the greatest of all failures in the modern Evangelical church. We have broached this topic already, but here it would be useful, I believe, to examine in more detail exactly what the Scriptures teach on this topic, and to "drill down" even deeper on just why this issue is so vital. For if we fail to ascertain its full significance, the work of prayer, I fear, will continue to fall by the wayside.

The Bible teaches that the Holy Spirit is God himself; he is presented in the Word of God as equal to the Father and the Son in essence and glory (Matt 28:19; 2 Cor 13:14). Furthermore, it is he who is the source of all spiritual life (John 6:63); it is he who causes dead souls to be born again (John 3:5–8). It is by his power alone that we can put sin to death (Rom 8:13). It is by him alone that we can bear any fruit of holiness (Gal 5:16ff). It is he who has distributed spiritual gifts to the church (1 Cor 12:7–11). And it is through his power that we will ultimately conquer sin, death and hell, and rise again to glorious and uninterrupted fellowship with God the Father (Rom 8:9–11).

And it is him to whom we are constantly directed in the New Testament. We are to set our minds on the things of the Spirit (Rom 8:5), walk by the Spirit (Gal 5:16), be led by the Spirit (Gal 5:18), be filled with the Spirit (Eph 5:18), pray in the Spirit (Eph 6:18), and put sin to death by the Spirit (Rom 8:13). We are to preserve the unity of the Spirit (Eph 4:3) and be careful not to grieve the Spirit away (Eph 4:30).

Clearly, then, our entire being, for all of our lives, is to be, for lack of a better term—but in fact I think it is the most appropriate term—*consumed* by the Spirit of God. And in the great duty that is required of us—to love God with all of our being, and pour out our lives in loving sacrifice to him—we must understand that we can only do this to the degree that we know the power and influence of his Spirit in our lives.

A great question all believers must face and answer is simply this: are we truly aware of our need of the Spirit? A second, more pressing question is this: do we truly desire the Spirit's influence in our lives? I believe that many of us have at least a vague awareness of our need of the Spirit, but perhaps not as we ought. We must come to grips with the fact that we can do no spiritually good thing—*nothing*—unless we are empowered by the Spirit of God. We must be under the influence of his affections, feelings, and desires—his power—if we are to do anything good in the sight of God at any time. And if we are for a moment without him, then we are setting ourselves up for sin; indeed, we have no hope of resisting it at all.

I am not suggesting here that these things are always easy to understand; nor does the Bible unpack for us, of course, exactly how this all works out. The Bible is largely silent, in the end, on exact details about our makeup as creatures, as we have said. The same could be said of the influence of the Spirit of God upon us. The one thing we can be sure of from the biblical record is that the Holy Spirit's influence produces obvious effects, both in our emotions and in our deeds; and there is little doubt that both his presence and his absence can be felt.

But what about the second question? Perhaps the greatest problem regarding the Spirit in the church today is not abuse—which Baptists and Presbyterians often accuse Pentecostals and Charismatics of—but neglect. Since the attacks of modernism in the nineteenth century there has been an emphasis in Evangelical circles on a proper valuing of the Word of God, and for this we are thankful. I trust that many of us do not need to be convinced of the utter necessity and significance of God's Word. But what about the Spirit? In churches where the Word of God is central, have we neglected the Holy Spirit? Have we forgotten that by itself, the Word of God can do nothing? That only by the Spirit can we understand it (1 Cor 2:14), believe it (John 6:63–65), and obey it (Rom 8:4–13)? Have we forgotten that the Spirit is that being by whom we are to wield the weapon of the Word of God through prayer, and that without it we simply cannot fight against sin and the devil (Eph 6:17)?

Many in the Evangelical world, especially in the Reformed community, do not seem to believe anymore that the Spirit is a living being with real, experiential power (Acts 1:8). They seem to forget that by him men of old overcame fear and weakness and witnessed boldly of Christ, time and again (Acts 4:8, 4:31, 7:55, etc.) They seem to forget that by him glorious miracles were accomplished (Acts 2:4; 5:12; 6:8). They seem to think that all of this has somehow ceased in our day. And even if we believe that some of the so-called extraordinary gifts of the Spirit are not as prevalent in our day as they were in the early church, or that they have ceased altogether, then how about other, more "ordinary" works of the Spirit? His power to help us love God, or put sin to death, or pray? Even though some churches claim to believe that the Spirit alone can empower these, they certainly do not behave as if they do.

The Reformed community seems to have let the abuses of the Holy Spirit in our day run us to an opposite extreme. There are indeed those in our day who seek the Holy Spirit not out of love to God, or out of concern for his glory, but for personal gain and power, like Simon of old (Acts 8:17ff). They seek the wonders of the Spirit, but have not the graces. They seek the power of the Spirit, but have not his presence in their daily lives. They demonstrate little or nothing of his real fruits, yet they claim, to the sad destruction of many, to have his gifts and authority. Such charlatans continue to flourish in our day, and their sanctuaries are for the most part perverse, pleasure-seeking, demonically-infested catacombs of fanaticism and heresy. They preach little or nothing of biblical truth. They know little or nothing of the real meaning of the cross. The know little of true holiness, the very thing by which the Spirit is named. They emphasize a spirit of joy, victory, and power, but it is not of God. They profess to work miracles, speak in tongues, and see visions, and yet they know little of the Spirit's power over daily sin. They have a power, all right, but it may very well be the dark and destructive power of the forces of wickedness.

Such abuses might cause anyone to shy away from talk of the Spirit; but again I say, we must not let such rob us of his glorious presence. We must understand that he is absolutely essential, and we must give ourselves over to seeking him. For the Spirit will not give himself to those who seek him out of wrong motives, but neither will he give himself to those who do not seek him at all. God calls us to give our all to him—and perhaps the most foundational way we are to do this is to give ourselves over to seeking his Spirit's presence in our lives.

We can know the Spirit's power, if only we ask for it (Luke 11:13)—and yet I say again, we will never know his power if we do not ask for it. Though our God grants us his power daily, far beyond what we are even aware of—out of sheer mercy, grace, and love—the greater filling and power of the Spirit will not be won without a battle. Though it may seem paradoxical, again, we must deny ourselves and take up our crosses daily just to know the Spirit's grace and help to do so more and more. For the flesh is in opposition to the things of the Spirit (Rom 8:5ff), and it will not be put to death without a real struggle.

Our God has called us to follow him for all of our days, but he is not in the business of carrying us along. All is by grace indeed; but the first input of grace in our lives, I believe, is meant to drive us to the difficult, bloody work of killing the flesh and giving ourselves over to seeking God through the means of prayer. We will never be carried over and around this struggle, for in it, I believe we can say with confidence, God is truly glorified.

Again, here are the questions we all must answer: do we really want the Spirit's power in our lives? Do we really want to love God, serve God, be holy, be his witnesses, and know the marvelous joy of intimate communion with him? Do we really want to see him glorified in the world? Is there any life or heart for such things at all within us? Is there even a flicker of interest, affection, and zeal for God? Then we must by all means build upon it.

A REFLECTION

My friend, have you ever truly known the grace and power of the Holy Spirit in your life? Have you ever been filled so marvelously, so unspeakably gloriously, with love to God and our Lord Jesus Christ, that you felt your soul was going to burst? Have you ever so *felt* for God, and been so ignited with a real, burning passion for his glory and honor in the world, that you longed to pour out your very life in all-out sacrifice for his name, no matter what the cost? Has zeal for God ever consumed you? Have you ever known such joy in your heart, such a mysterious, other-worldly, pulse-quickening joy, that you longed to cast off the bonds of flesh and join the glorious multitude around the throne? Has the sweet, strong presence of the Spirit ever left you with an incredible longing? Has time with God ever left you yearning for more, and deeper, and truer, fellowship with him? Have you ever been so full of the Spirit, that the lusts of the flesh, which have so often held you in their grip, seemed foul, detestable, and powerless? Have you ever been so filled with love to God that the very thought of sin was repugnant and heart-wrenchingly grievous to you? Have you ever obeyed God simply out of the love you truly felt for him? Have you ever turned away from the pleasures of the flesh and the world simply out of sheer delight in the things of God? Has his Word ever seemed more beautiful, more precious, and more alluring, than all other joys and entertainments? Have you ever felt such joy in the beauty and majesty of Christ that the delights of earth, even those that are natural and wholesome, seemed bland and empty? Have you ever known the Spirit's power in witness and testimony? Have you ever known God's help so strongly in some encounter that you knew for one divine moment that he had used you? Have you ever been swept into the very throne room of heaven on the wings of Spirit-empowered prayer?

These are the experiences that await us; these are those that are promised to us. The Spirit of God *longs* to consume us. He is, after all, a divine energy—a passionate, irresistible power. He is, we could say, the essence of God himself, the very heartbeat of God, a flame of eternal love. He is the great source of all spiritual life. And he longs to fill us to the full with the glorious presence and power of God the Father. When this happens in our lives, the presence of God will become so real, that earth itself will seem an illusion. The fear of God will flood our minds and hearts. The love of God in Christ will overwhelm and thrill us. The joy of God will well up like a titanic wave and threaten to burst our souls. The Word of God will become in our grasp a victorious weapon. We will roar in the Devil's face and bid him flee. We will sweep temptation aside as if by a mighty gale. We will tread the path of holiness with firm, sure steps, and all who see us will know our God is real.

Do we really want this in our lives? Then I say again, we must seek it. God longs to fill us with his glorious presence; he has commanded us to be entirely given over in love to him, and he is ready to strengthen us to obey him. He wants us to love and long for his glory as he himself does; and he yearns to bring us into that glorious, divine fellowship that he himself enjoys. How in the world can we not seek this? How in the world can we not desire to fulfill this grand calling?

The Word of God makes it clear that all of God's true people will indeed desire this, and seek it; for he has promised to pour out the Spirit upon all who are truly his (John 7:38). This is not only our grand calling, but it is our ultimate destiny as true Christians—both here on earth, and on that day when we arrive in heaven. For on that glorious day when we see the Lord, I believe we can say with certainty that all who loved and sought the Lord and his Spirit on earth will finally know the full and complete outpouring of his Spirit within them, with bodies recreated for that glorious purpose. And then all the love, longing, joy, and hope that we have known in part on earth, will at last be all fulfilled—as we are finally and fully consumed by the Spirit of the living God, to our infinite delight, and his eternal praise.

THE SPIRIT-FILLED LIFE

It has been my experience that those who are filled with the Spirit of God are increasingly willing to give up anything and everything—even the natural enjoyments and pleasures of life on earth—to see God's Spirit fill them even more. Such a person will not necessarily see earthly enjoyments as sinful in themselves, or deny himself out of guilt or an inappropriate sense of duty; on the contrary, he will be able to take part in wholesome recreational activities with complete freedom of conscience, for the refreshment, restoration, and enjoyment of his mind and body. Whatever is sinless of the old realm, which awaits renewal—nature and man's own recreation of it in the visual arts, the joys of language, music, society, even sport—the Spirit-filled soul can yet love and enjoy these every bit as much as Adam, and these will go with us into the New Age. We must not get so carried away with our heavenly vision that we forget that we have bodies, and are destined always to have them; and so always to enjoy a world of the senses. The Bible is clear on this. But we must never make the mistake—the great mistake—of prioritizing or choosing the Old World over the New, or of thinking that the path to heaven leads back to Eden. For we are no longer Adam—we are united to Christ. Something greater has come. Even our enjoyment of sensuous things in the world to come will be in a new way and on a heretofore-unknown level; at the very least, we know from Scripture that God will be the center and sum of our delights in a way that we can scarcely imagine on earth. And this the Spirit-filled man begins more and more to anticipate.

And thus the Spirit-filled soul will enjoy the things of earth, and yet he will inevitably feel the great press and weight of neglecting God, and of wasting time that could have been spent promoting God's kingdom and glory—which are yet to be fully realized. He will begin to feel more and more the magnitude of what loving God with all his heart, soul, mind, and strength really means, and thus his grand desire will be to devote more and more of himself, and more and more of his time, to the very person of God—until the totality of his being and his life are truly given over to God and his things. It is vital to emphasize that as the Spirit's influence expands and deepens in person's life, that person will no longer be *inclined* toward the things of earth. The palate of his soul will no longer be satisfied with the bland and finite scraps of earth; he will long more and more for the infinitely ravishing joys of God, Christ, heaven, and spiritual things, and he will seek these above all else. Let us make no mistake: the Spirit-filled man is drawn toward heaven, toward full and unhindered communion with God himself. We will remain bodies, indeed, throughout eternity, but bodies recreated for the glorious purpose of loving God utterly, and acting always out of unadulterated zeal for him, by the power of his Spirit, in whatever task he calls us to in the New Heaven and the New Earth.

God help us, then, in this whole matter of seeking his Spirit. It is, again, our great calling and destiny. But there are yet other matters to speak of. For when a man truly begins to be given over to the Spirit of God, he will begin to discover an entirely new world. For he will be lifted beyond earthly things into a real and deadly serious realm—the realm of the spiritual. And there he will discover that a colossal and deadly serious war is waging, a war between the forces of good and evil; and there he will discover that he is fighting for the glory of God on a whole new level, against powers of evil that will challenge and threaten him to the uttermost. And though his life and indeed his very soul are threatened, it is in this realm that the truly Spirit-filled man will strive to dwell and conquer, for he will come quickly to understand that until his time on earth is done, this world is the only one that matters.

SPIRITUAL WARFARE: THE UNSEEN REALITY

There is an unseen battle that rages. The Word of God makes it clear that beyond the scope of ordinary human perception, and over and above all earthly affairs, pursuits, and interests—and yet intimately concerned with the lives of men—there is a furious, never-ceasing, all-out war taking place between the forces of God and the forces of evil. Each and every human being in fully involved in this conflict, whether they know it or not, and each is fighting either for God or against him. At stake are the glory of God and the destinies of all men.

The Christian is called to this battle most clearly in Ephesians 6:10 and following, where we are told that our battle is against the "powers, against the world forces of this darkness, against the spiritual forces of wickedness in the heavenly places." Evil spiritual beings exist who long to rob God of his glory by disrupting his purposes and hindering the advancement of his kingdom. A chief way they seek to do so is by causing his vessels on earth to grow weak and sin. To accomplish this, they will attack every aspect of their spiritual lives, as the passage above makes clear: they will attack their love, faith, purity, hope, and peace, and they will not rest until the battle is won or lost.

Every true Christian, whose life is coming more and more under the control of the Spirit, knows something of this battle. He begins to feel the devil's attacks and learns to take seriously the injunctions of the Apostle Paul to take up the full armor of God (Eph 6:10ff). He learns that the sole source of his power is indeed the Spirit of God, which wields the Word of God as a weapon. And he learns that victory will only come through the means of Spirit-empowered prayer.

Here is the passage in full:

> Finally, be strong in the Lord and in the strength of His might. Put on the full armor of God, so that you will be able to stand firm against the schemes of the devil. For our struggle is not against flesh and blood, but against the rulers, against the powers, against the world forces of this darkness, against the spiritual forces of wickedness in the heavenly places. Therefore, take up the full armor of God, so that you will be able to resist in the evil day, and having done everything, to stand firm. Stand firm therefore, having girded your loins with truth, and having put on the breastplate of righteousness, and having shod your feet with the preparation of the gospel of peace; in addition to all, taking up the shield of faith with which you will be able to

extinguish all the flaming arrows of the evil one. And take the helmet of salvation, and the sword of the Spirit, which is the word of God. With all prayer and petition pray at all times in the Spirit, and with this in view, be on the alert with all perseverance and petition for all the saints, and pray on my behalf, that utterance may be given to me in the opening of my mouth, to make known with boldness the mystery of the gospel, for which I am an ambassador in chains; that in proclaiming it I may speak boldly, as I ought to speak (Eph 6:10-20).

From verses 10 to 17a, Paul enjoins us to take up and put on the various elements of defense. Then we are told in verse 17b that the weapon we are given to attack with is the Word of God, which is called here the "sword of the Spirit." Clearly, then, the Word of God is to be wielded by means of the Spirit. And how are we to do this? The passage is clear: we are to "pray at all times in the Spirit," being "alert with all perseverance and petition for all the saints" (verse 18). Our chief method for wielding the weapon of the Word of God in our lives is prayer, for prayer is the means by which we obtain the Spirit's power.

Therefore we must beseech God in Spirit-empowered prayer to grant us strength, that we might cast down the forces of sin and darkness in our lives and in the world. We cannot merely speak the Word of God over such forces, waving it as some sort of magic wand of faith, as is claimed by some today; we must pray and plead with God daily to work it out in our lives, and to establish his will and purpose in the world. For the power of his Spirit is the world's only hope.

This is indeed what we see the saints of God doing all throughout the Bible. In the verses we examined above—and there are many more examples—the people of God depended on the power of God for every spiritual good, through the means of prayer. For they knew that "the effective prayer of a righteous man can accomplish much" (Jas 5:16). They knew the words of the Lord Jesus, that the forces of evil are often so strong that they can only be defeated by means of extraordinary prayer (Mark 9:29). They knew, as Paul did, that the prayers of the saints played a vital and even necessary part in the accomplishment of the will of God (2 Cor 1:11). And they knew, again, that such prayer was their only hope in the great spiritual conflict of which they were a part, as Ephesians 6 makes clear.

Do we really know anything of this conflict? Do we know anything of prayer in the Spirit (Jude 20)? Are our prayers conformed to the Word of God, and do we pray according to the truths and promises contained therein? And are we striving to pray continually and incessantly, as we are commanded, knowing that such is our only hope? Do we seek to set aside extraordinary times of prayer, and couple prayer with fasting? Do we truly realize that we can accomplish no spiritual good without the help of God's Spirit? Do we understand that we cannot defeat the forces of evil to any degree without the power of God?

This warfare is indeed intense and deadly serious, but the problem is that most professing Christians in our day are far from the front lines. The professing Christian church today knows little of what Paul is talking about. The devil is indeed raging with all his power, but he is often not raging directly against the professing church. For many church members today, I fear, are not truly in the battle. They do not realize it, but they are still fighting on the side of the enemy. They are still "held captive" by the devil, "to do his will" (2 Timothy 2:26). They are not really living for God; indeed, they are fighting against him. For they have not been truly born again.

I contend, however, that the genuine Christian inevitably finds himself in the middle of this conflict, almost before he even knows it. As the Spirit works out such things as purity, humility, love to others, and consistent, Spirit-led prayer in his life, he begins to fall under attack. He learns that our great enemy, Satan, is hindered when we pray to God in the Spirit; he knows that God works against him and his schemes when we do so. And when the Christian is used by God in prayer, all the forces of darkness turn against him. All-out war is declared, and he is attacked on every side. Temptations, trials, disappointments, aggravations, and even sickness are among the many things that are hurled his way, more intensely than ever before. The purpose of it all is to cause him to sin in some way or to lose heart, and ultimately to dishonor the name of God. As the book of Job indicates, as well as Jesus's words to Peter in Luke 22:31, the devil pleads with God for such access to us, and often God grants it. He grants it because we must learn to be Christian soldiers; we must learn that we are in a war, and that God wants us to wage it, and to fight it, for his glory. He wants us to stand strong in purity and prayer, and to win the victory. He wants us by the strength of his might to stand firm against the schemes of the devil in the evil day, for in this he is glorified.

And yet I say again that the Christian church today knows little of this reality, and again I declare that it is because many of us are still fighting on the wrong side. The devil does not attack his own. He does not wage war against his own forces. He provides for them and grants their wishes, that they might continue to do his bidding and help accomplish his purpose—the dishonor of God and the robbery of his glory. And yet, for some Christians, the possibility exists that they are not yet fully aware of the battle that is waging all around them. But the Word of God makes it clear that this struggle is not some addendum to the Christian life—it is not a war waged on a far distant front by Christian soldiers carefully selected and trained for that purpose. My friend, if you are a true follower of Christ, you will soon discover that you are in this conflict. You have been shoved right into the middle of a real war, and you had better grab your weapons and get to praying. You had better plead with God to grant you spiritual strength to overcome all sin and weakness, and all the forces of hell, and to "stand firm." And you had better get to praying for all the saints, for many of your brethren in the world today are under all-out attack and are threatened to be destroyed, and perhaps will be—at least physically—unless someone pleads with God on their behalf (2 Thess 3:1–2).

Are the purposes of God firm, and never able to be thwarted? Of course they are. The devil cannot do many things, such as separate us from the love of Christ (Rom 8:31ff), and he can do nothing at all unless God allows it. Such books as Job make it clear that Satan can do nothing without the express allowance of almighty God. But here is a sober truth, and one that the church of God in our day had better come to grips with: it is the will of God to allow his people to experience real, deadly-serious warfare, and even at times to be seriously wounded and defeated, if only for a while. Again, when our Lord Jesus told Peter that the devil had obtained permission from God to sift him like wheat, apparently only the prayers of our Lord Jesus Christ himself prevented him from completely falling away. What an incredibly sobering passage this is, and it is perhaps because of this episode that Peters warn us later to "Be of sober spirit, be on the alert. Your adversary, the devil, prowls around like a roaring lion, seeking someone to devour" (1 Pet 5:8). Our God wants to stir us up to fight. He wants us to take up our weapons in the power of the Spirit and wage war for his glory. He wants us to overcome sin and defeat the devil, and he wants to see his kingdom progress, his church built up, and lost souls saved for his glory. He wants the light of his gospel to advance and his word to speed ahead and be glorified (2 Thess 3:1).

I contend that the devil fights most strongly against intercession. If the battle is the Lord's, and if it is by his power that we will accomplish the victory, and if that power comes uniquely through the means of prayer, then serious, persistent prayer is that thing that Satan will strive most earnestly to defeat. And this has been my experience and the experience of numerous saints in days gone by. If you are attempting to pray, then wherever you are weakest, the devil will attack. He is ingenious in his methods, and once he gets a "foothold," as those of a bygone generation were fond of saying, then the only thing one can do is ride it out and beg for mercy. This is why watchfulness is key. But there is no question that we will be defeated at times. When I attempted to set up the prayer meeting at the local church campus I mentioned previously, the devil afflicted me with a mysterious sickness, and all but silenced me for weeks at a time in my attempt to pray. Worry, fear, or just plain illness, leading to worry and fear; inexplicable disagreements that somehow spiral out of control and result in hurt that can last for days; you name it, the devil will use it, and he knows just when to strike. He can get in our heads or in-between our closest relationships in a moment. That's why we must bring in others to assist us. Only together, perhaps, can we defeat this great enemy.

Are we consistent enough in our prayer lives to intercede for all the saints? Is our prayer life sufficiently developed, and are we filled enough with the Spirit of God to wage war on behalf of others—especially those who are engaged in full-time ministry? Are we truly able to heed the biblical exhortations and commands to do so? Are we aware of the great struggle, the great conflict, that many Christians face in our day? Are we truly aware of the battle that rages? We cannot save men, and neither can the devil ultimately prevent their salvation, but both of us have a hand, however mysterious it may seem, in the outcome. The devil will do everything he can to rob God of his glory and prevent his purposes, but we can thwart the purposes of the devil, and play a part in the success of the purposes of God—if only by his grace we are able to pray!

We must rise up and seek the living God. We must become people of righteous, fervent, consistent, Spirit-empowered prayer. We must be those who give up the passing pursuits of earth and give ourselves to extraordinary prayer, even prayer and sacrificial offerings to God such as fasting, no matter how difficult and painful they may be. We must be those who wage real war, and know real victory, through effectual prayer. We must grow and increase in this grace and work, and with God's help do it all the more. May we be those who battle day after day for the people and purposes of God, and for the salvation of perishing sinners around the world! May we become true soldiers of the cross. For our God has called us to it, and as we have said, all true Christians are indeed involved in this war, whether they fully comprehend it or not.

We are either helping the purposes of God or hindering them. We are either winning glorious battles for Christ or losing them. There is no middle ground. There are no lulls in this battle; there are no ceasefires. There will be no truce. The devil will rage until the war is won, and so must we. May God help us to rise up and pray. May God help us to pray until we become genuinely holy people. May God help us to intercede with all our hearts for his church and for the souls of the lost. May God grant us more of his Spirit, and help us more and more to pray in his Spirit, until we see him glorified on the earth and his kingdom established. For such prayer, such warfare, is indeed a true measure of love to God; this is what it truly means to give heart, soul, mind, and strength for his glorious name.

I am convinced that a serious effort toward such Spirit-empowered prayer is *the church's last chance*. Not only is the Evangelical church incredibly weak in this area of prayer, but with the world getting all the more wicked and hostile and the foundations of church doctrine and practice crumbling all around, we really have no other choice. But the remarkable thing to consider is that it has always been this way. This kind of commitment to prayer has *always* been what is necessary to see God work. What, then, does this say about the church in our day? Where are the intercessors? Where are the prophetic voices calling us to prayer? Where is the Spirit of God? And if these are missing, can we really say with any degree of confidence that God is with us?

4

Mission

It was into a world of soon-to-be dissipating calm that my mother was born, in 1948. I have seen a few of her childhood pictures over the years, and I have always been struck by her appearance. She has her father's wide, prominent forehead, as well as his almost shockingly stark bone structure, deep set eyes, and aristocratic nose. He had been called a handsome man, and my mother's face was similarly pleasant to look at, if not a bit imposing. There are those, the saying goes, who wear their emotions on their sleeves; my mother did that, for sure, but she also wore her entire personality all over her face like a well-placed highway billboard. Even when she was a child, you could tell that she was strong-willed just by looking at her. The nearly indomitable personality that led her father to earthly greatness, however, was mixed in her female soul with her mother's combination of sensitivity and tenderness. Add to this the fact that my mother was born into a family that already had two boys, with whom she had a merry time keeping up, and the path to the complex soul she would remain throughout her life was set. She and her brothers did everything together, which was sometimes not a good thing. My grandfather was already a prosperous and rather distracted lawyer by the time she was old enough to have memories, and the three young children were often left to fend for themselves, in true rural American South style. How many dirt roads, fishing holes, and ramshackle country stores they frequented one can only imagine. My mother would later call herself a tomboy, and I came to understand this not only as a result of how she grew up, but of her natural inclinations. She was, as she would later confess, something of a mess as a child. She eschewed her mother's dresses and hair curlers for bare feet and football with the boys. Skinned knees, ticks, and hookworms were her frequent companions; but this was all just part of life in the rural South. Like many young children reared in similar circumstances, fictitious or otherwise, my mother's early experiences with school were pure horror, for her and her teachers. She always wanted to be outside, and besides, she couldn't sit still or concentrate. A generation or two later, she might have been diagnosed with ADHD, but in those days, there was nothing for a teacher to do but throw up her hands in despair. She spent countless hours isolated near the teacher's desk; one threatened to tie her to her chair. Finally, my mother recalls, one gentle, patient, rather angelic female teacher managed to keep her still and focused, and she won my mother's admiration for life.

But as soon as school let out, my mother and her brothers would be at it again. Mischief and misadventure seemed to be the order of the day. In one oft-told story, my mother and her brothers took to secretly smoking cigarettes in a weedy field near the house, sending Jay, the eldest, to the country store when supplies were low. How he managed to buy cigarettes as a young boy was never explained to me, but this was beside the point; the point of the story was that for my mother and her brothers, sin came as easily as sunshine on those Louisiana summer days. "Get Old Golds, Jay!" she yelled one afternoon, as her oldest brother headed back into town to replenish the stash. My grandfather, alerted by the rings of smoke rising among the weeds, had stridden over to rain judgment upon the evildoers, and he never failed to repeat this story, his personal favorite, with a chuckle. My mother was only five years old.

As the years went on, she did well enough in school, and she found herself popular at every stage of life, a fact no doubt attributable to her attractiveness and fun-loving personality, as well as to her father's burgeoning reputation; but she was beset with insecurities from an early age. Some of it, she would later tell me, was due to the easy-going success of her handsome and athletic second-oldest brother, Fox, the one just up from her in the family pecking order. Jay had learning disabilities and struggled at every stage, but Fox was the life of the party, and partied everywhere he went. According to my mother, he made A's without even trying, starred on the football field and the basketball court, and always dated the prettiest girls in town. The only thing he failed to do, apparently, was win his father's unconditional approval. Like so many other sons of that generation, he took his father's lack of acceptance hard, and rebelled against it. My mother, torn between her own admiration for Fox and her inability to keep up, watched in sadness over the years as their relationship deteriorated, but she felt that her own lack of accomplishment likewise failed to win her father's full approval, no matter how hard she tried to love and obey him, unlike Fox. It wasn't that her father didn't love her in his own way, and her mother certainly did; it was mostly that she felt her older sibling's superiority acutely, and this shaped her perception of herself for years afterward. Despite the challenges of these relationships over the years, however, both her father and her brother came to greatly respect and admire her for her Christian convictions, and in my memory her relationship with both was strong.

After her sophomore year in high school everything suddenly changed for my mother. Her father, John McKeithen, was elected governor of Louisiana in 1964. My mother went from the dirt roads and cotton fields of rural Louisiana to living in the opulent Louisiana governor's mansion for eight years, which boasted some eighteen bathrooms, servants at one's beck and call, and chauffeured limousines. It was the Beverly Hillbillies come to life. Before long, as queen of the Washington D.C. Mardi Gras ball, she was meeting the young and dashing Prince Charles—to whom she managed to blurt out the Four Spiritual Laws as he passed by in the greeting line—and dancing with Vice President Hubert Humphrey. Far beyond the glitz and glamour, however, there were two dramatic meetings in Baton Rouge that changed my mother's life forever. One was with Jesus; the other was with my father.

The first meeting, her true conversion, took the electric, imposing energy my mother has always had and channeled it into a one-woman witnessing crew for Jesus. She might as well have been the Campus Crusade poster child, rounding up hapless targets at rallies for Josh McDowell and acting out deliberate evangelistic charades to reach the lost. When she and my father met, they were both Christians, and something of Louisiana celebrities. When they married in 1972, it made state-wide news. Then on they went to the NFL. Then to the ministry. Then to obscurity. And then to the mission field, where she found herself, initially, with nothing to do. Here she was, a strong, confident, gifted woman who had spent the past nearly thirty years serving my father, raising children, and engaging in significant ministry in her own right. What was she to do? Had all of her labor alongside my father prepared her for nothing?

Would there be, in the end, a ministry for my mother, in the difficult Asian country they had landed in? As she prayed over these things, her heart began to be moved by the incredible number of street children in the town where we worked. Then she learned about unwanted babies given up for adoption. Then about orphans scattered here and there. And then about the countless numbers of abused and neglected women. And God began to move her heart.

Fast forward twenty-two years, to the present day. In her time in that country and afterward, God has used my mother's background, undeniable strengths, and all the lessons she had learned over the years to found an NPO that has helped hundreds of women, children, and families in the neediest countries of Asia. Right now, that NPO is engaged in a life-and-death struggle for the souls of orphans caught up in the civil war in Myanmar. Through the grace of Almighty God, my mother, the sensitive and insecure country girl from Louisiana, has blazed a trail of Spirit-empowered usefulness across several needy countries, albeit not without more lessons and humility learned along the way. Her life and legacy are a living example of a real and fruitful ministry, which, if it is to know God's real blessing, must be done in God's way, and in God's timing—the subject of this chapter.

THE QUESTION OF MISSION

The question before us now is "What is the church to do?" Having established the absolute necessity of prayer, and having presented prayer in the Spirit as the great work to which all Christians are called, we are not, of course, arguing that this is *all* Christians should be doing. It is certainly what they should begin doing, or should do first; the example of Acts 13:2, in which the gathered were serving God and fasting, that extraordinary manifestation of one's need for God, is certainly instructive. I will argue, in fact, that doing one's ordinary duty in the context of the local church, and waiting on God in prayer, is how the Holy Spirit selects and sends out souls for gospel ministry (verses 2–4). Prayer is, indeed, the foundational work of the Great Commission. But the point here is that in addition to holiness and prayer, God has a unique ministry for each of his people. And this ministry is to be a God-appointed part of God's purpose in the world, his *mission*.

The word "mission," to be sure, has become something of a catchphrase, especially when associated with God—the so-called *missio Dei*, or mission of God. This phrase began to gather steam in the twentieth century, and today, whatever the complexities of the discussion in days gone by, the "mission of God" is popularly explained as follows: "God's mission is accomplished through his Son's life, death, and resurrection. His mission is to save us from our sins and to restore his good creation which had been marred by sin."[1] If we are reading such statements right, then, God's mission involves these two things: *redemption* and *restoration*. Again, this sort of understanding of the mission of God seems commonplace, and the application for Christians is inevitably the same: we must align ourselves with the mission of God, and engage ourselves in his grand mission of redeeming mankind. Mostly, that is, we should engage in "missions."

PROBLEMS WITH THE "REDEMPTION MODEL"

It is not the purpose of this book to get sidetracked by philosophical theology to any great degree, but I can't help but mention in passing here that there are problems lurking about this popular presentation of God's mission, problems that should at least be considered. An initial problem is that the claim is rather hopelessly ambiguous. Consider, first, the claim itself:

> (1) God's mission is to redeem and restore his creation,

where "creation" includes all that God has made, including humanity. But now notice, by comparison:

> (1a) God's mission is to redeem and restore *all* of his creation.

Does (1) imply (1a)? It is not clear that it does, but it is clear that it could. But (1a) implies universalism, the idea that God will ultimately redeem all people, which is not a biblical idea, and thus not one that Evangelicals can accept. Perhaps, though, (1a) can be amended. Consider, then, the following:

> (1b) God's mission is to redeem and restore *as much of his creation as he can*.

---

1. Akin and Ashford, *Going*, 8.

The most obvious supporters of (1b), of course, would be those who hold to a libertarian version of free will. Libertarian free will is the popular version of free will, the one the man on the street is likely to hold. It says that man's actions are not determined, or forced, by God or anything else; all of man's choices are fully under his control, he is free to choose among them, and he is thereby responsible for them.[2] Christians who believe in this kind of free will argue that God's power is limited only by man's free will, which God has created mankind with. If God's purpose in redemption fails for some or even most of mankind—that is, if not everyone will be saved—then it is simply because of God's larger purpose, which is to achieve the great good of some souls choosing him *freely*. God is truly doing all he can, but he is dependent, by his decree, on man's free will, both to choose God in salvation and to take the gospel to others who need it.

Libertarian free will, indeed, is the view of free will that many Evangelical Christians have. We have already discussed some problems associated with this view, but I think it will be useful to go a bit further into this discussion here, especially since the passion of many church members on this topic seems to far outstrip their knowledge. First of all, as is widely known in the philosophical and theological communities, the notion of libertarian free will is fraught with difficulty, the most well-known problem being the simple matter of causation; if choices are not determined, or made necessary, by any cause, then these choices, it would seem, must be random, and therefore beyond an agent's control. Philosopher Robert Kane puts it this way:

> If free will is not compatible with determinism, it does not seem to be compatible with indeterminism either. The arguments to show this have been made since ancient times. An undetermined or chance event, it is said, occurs spontaneously and is not controlled by anything, hence not controlled by the agent.[3]

Various theories have been put forth to seek to combat this problem, but, as Kane notes again:

> Persons who believe free choices cannot be determined (as libertarians do) must say [a person] may have chosen different possible futures, given the same entire past, including his psychological and physical history up to the moment he did choose.

---

2. Libertarianism is more traditionally defined as "being able to do otherwise than one does in any given situation."

3. Kane, "Libertarianism," 23.

And this does seem to make his choosing otherwise (choosing Colorado) arbitrary and irrational in the same circumstances in which he actually came to favor Hawaii and chose it. You can see why many people have argued that undetermined free choices, of the kind libertarians demand, would be "arbitrary," "capricious," "random," "irrational," "uncontrolled," and "inexplicable," and not really free and responsible choices at all.

Defenders of libertarian free will, according to their critics, have a dismal record of answering such charges.[4]

It is hard to see, really, how this situation could improve. But there are other philosophical problems with libertarian free will. For one, no clear or definitive account of it has ever been given. The same cannot be said of theories of human action that are not libertarian; indeed, the model we mentioned previously, of the primacy of human desire or passion and its role in directing choices, is perfectly explanatory of human behavior; humans are led by their strongest or most immediate passions, and the choices of the will are determined by them. And for many thinkers, such a view of human behavior is in fact compatible with free will, or can even be seen as a species of free will—hence the popularity of *compatibilism* in philosophical and theological circles, which denotes the view that free will and determinism can both be true at the same time.

And there are still other problems with the libertarian free will approach, especially as related to the matter of God's mission. One might reasonably ask, indeed, if God has done or is doing *all that he possibly can* to see people saved. God could, it seems, do much more to stop lost people from dying, or to facilitate the spread of the gospel, without violating or otherwise compromising anyone's free will. But here, perhaps, we are going a bit too far afield. Indeed, this whole discussion leads to several thorny but incredibly important issues related to the attributes of God, as well as the problems of sin, suffering, and hell. It pushes us, indeed, to the problem of evil and theodicy, where we are compelled to defend our belief in God in the face of what appear to be lapses or failures in his divine goodness, knowledge, or omnipotence. But surely enough philosophical ink has been spilled on this topic already. The main issue here is what the Scriptures teach on the matter of free will and the mission of God.

That the Bible presents human beings as having choices is clear; that human beings are generally responsible for their choices is also clear. However, many theologians would argue that the sovereignty of God in

4. Kane, "Libertarianism," 24.

salvation is equally clear in the Bible; specifically, that God's grace is both *necessary* and *sufficient* for salvation, and also that he has some people that he chooses to save (the elect) and some he doesn't. For the holder of these doctrines, then, neither (1), (1a), or (1b) are adequate. What we need, then, is something like (1c):

> (1c) God's mission is to redeem and restore those whom he has sovereignly chosen to redeem and restore.

But here we are immediately faced with problems of a different sort. What then shall we make of those whom God has *not* chosen to redeem and restore? For what purpose do they exist? Clearly, then, we are being pushed toward another direction altogether. For if there are those whom God has created but has chosen not to redeem, then it seems that for the one who believes in the sovereignty of God over all things, (1c) is as unsatisfying as the others. For though it might describe *a* mission of God, or *one of* God's missions, it certainly cannot be descriptive of God's *larger* or *ultimate* purpose for the world. And, in fact, the Bible does seem to make it very plain, in such passages as Romans 9, that God creates some people not for redemption at all, but in order to demonstrate his power in them (verse 17). At the very least, then, (1c) is limited in scope; and this, I contend, compels us to more carefully consider this whole notion of "the mission of God."

GOD'S ULTIMATE PURPOSE AS THE CHURCH'S TRUE MISSION

It is certainly not my intention to argue, by any means, that redemption and restoration are not part of God's mission at all, or that God has no mission or purpose at all that relates to these things. What I am going to argue here, however, is that Christians should be wary when talk of God's mission in the redemptive sense—call it the redemption model—becomes too dominant or is overemphasized, such that it is viewed as God's—and the church's—ultimate and thus most important purpose. Certainly, God might have multiple purposes, some of which are "ultimate," and some which aren't;[5] some, indeed, might even be temporary. In the Old Testament, it was his mission, clearly, to rescue Noah and his

---

5. Of course, this line of thinking is thoroughly pursued by Edwards in the opening section of *The End for Which God Created the World*.

family from the flood, and in a sense to recreate the world; or, later, to free Israel from bondage and deliver them to the promised land. And it is certainly God's mission now for the church to make disciples of all nations. But if it can be established from Scripture that there is a larger or ultimate purpose in all that God does, that incorporates everything that has happened and is presently happening in the world, then I believe we would do well to align our own hearts with that purpose above all. And as we will see, I believe there is such an ultimate purpose.

No doubt, some theologians would be quick to point out that this "ultimate" notion of mission is not necessarily what is intended by *missio Dei*. "Mission," they have taught us, has to do with the whole notion of being *sent*, as the origin of the word indicates; thus it only applies to the work of redemption, restoration, missions, etc. that God has undertaken. God, in fact, may have other or indeed larger "missions" or purposes that he is about. But my main complaint here, really, is just this: most *missio Dei* language today fails to capture God's ultimate aim or goal—while appearing for all intents and purposes to present it! The whole idea of "God's mission," again, has become a driving, even organizing and centering force in the church, and it inevitably comes back to these notions of redemption and restoration, with the resulting application that we should all engage in such purposes ourselves. Interestingly and somewhat disappointingly, even among those who argue, as I am here, that the notion of mission must somehow capture not just "missions," but something larger and greater, the amended notion still smacks of missions, and inevitably turns to talk of God's redemption and our involvement in it.[6]

Thus, my claim here, stated again as simply as possible, is this: if God has an *ultimate purpose* for all things, then the church must align itself first and foremost with that purpose. In other words, whatever ultimate aim, goal, or end God had for creating the world, should be what is emphasized above anything else in the church. My argument for this claim is largely intuitive, but I think compelling: first, whatever ultimate purpose God had for creating the world, is still his ultimate purpose; for God cannot change, and that purpose is obviously not yet fully accomplished. Second, if we are to be like God in the sense that we must passionately pursue what he passionately pursues—which I take to be undeniable from Scripture—then we must align ourselves first and foremost with what he is most passionate about. Let me state the matter another

---

6. See, for example, Wright, *Mission*, 22–23.

way: if there is indeed to be found in Scripture a grand or ultimate passion in the heart of God, and if it is indeed our duty to make this our own passion, then the church must discover what this is, and focus on this as its ultimate and overarching purpose and pursuit.

But is there, in fact, such a grand motivation in the heart of God? Does Scripture speak of a larger purpose for the world than redemption and restoration? I believe that it does. And to this truth—which, I contend, all Christians must honestly face and consider—we now turn.

GOD'S ULTIMATE MISSION: HIS OWN GLORY

What all Christians must come to grips with, I believe, is that it is clear in Scripture that God's ultimate purpose is not merely to redeem a portion of humanity, or restore his creation; his purpose, it turns out, is to *glorify himself*. In seeking to understand this notion, we can do better than to point back to Jonathan Edwards, whose views John Piper in our own day has perhaps worked hardest to promulgate.[7] As Edwards puts it: "Thus we see that the great end of God's works, which is so variously expressed in Scripture, is indeed but one; and this one end is most properly and comprehensively called, THE GLORY OF GOD."[8] And more specifically: "Thus it appears reasonable to suppose, that it was God's last end, that there might be a glorious and abundant emanation of his infinite fullness of good ad extra, or without himself; and that the disposition to communicate himself, or diffuse his own FULLNESS, was what moved him to create the world."[9] For Edwards, then, God's ultimate purpose is that his fullness, or the totality of his knowledge, excellency, and happiness,[10] be demonstrated outside of himself, to creatures that might come to share and delight in all that he is, and thus reflect God's own greatness back to him. And since God's happiness consists first and foremost in himself, Edwards says, directing creatures likewise to be happy in him is not antithetical to God's ultimate end, but one with it; for in their ultimate happiness in God, God is happy.[11]

---

7. Most notably in his *God's Passion for His Glory*.
8. Edwards, *Dissertation*, 60.
9. Edwards, *Dissertation*, 14.
10. Edwards, *Dissertation*, 15.
11. Edwards, *Dissertation*, 61.

The various complexities of these notions aside, for the purpose of clarity, my primary point here is simple: for Edwards and other Reformers, God's ultimate aim in creation is clearly "God-centered." In creating, sustaining, and presently working in the world, God aims to demonstrate his own glory, or show just how glorious he is. And this clearly moves us beyond redemption and restoration, for it must include the display of the *totality* of his character, including his justice. The following, then, becomes the Reformed explanation of the realities of judgment and damnation, as Matthew J. Hart puts it: "Important aspects of the divine majesty are not displayed if everyone is saved, so God decrees that many shall refuse his offer of salvation in order that, as the Westminster Confession mentions, the glories of his sovereign power and justice might be displayed in their eternal destruction."[12]

Again, if such notions are really supported in Scripture, then God's ultimate purpose is to glorify himself by displaying the full range of his attributes, not merely to redeem humanity. But, in the end, does the Bible support what Edwards is arguing for here? One would be hard-pressed not to think so. A study of verses on this issue in both the Old and New Testaments reveals an overwhelming emphasis on the God-centeredness of God, and on his glory being his ultimate aim in all things. But since the evidence is set forth so thoroughly in chapter two of Edwards's *The End for Which God Created the World*, one can only recommend a perusal of this evidence as it is gathered there to the reader.[13] Several things emerge from perusal of the evidence: (1) Generally speaking, the emphasis on God's glory in the Scriptures as his motivation for all things is strong, even compelling; (2) As we just said, in the Bible God aims to get glory for himself *in a wide variety of circumstances*, and not just in redemption strictly considered. As Edwards shows from the Scriptures, God works for his own glory in the things which he has made; in his sustaining of his creation; in all that comes to pass by his providence, including his judgments; in the preaching of the gospel; in the redemption of his people; in the sanctification of his church; etc. What emerges, then, is a picture of a God who is not only working for his glory in all things in the world, but who is working in a variety of arenas, so to speak, and who has a larger, broader purpose than simply redemption and restoration. For those who

---

12. Hart, "Calvinism," 250.

13. For those who cannot wait, a simple search of the phrase "glory of God" in the Bible reveals just how pervasive this idea is.

have yet to fully consider this evidence in the Word of God, Edwards's presentation of it is strongly recommended.

THE MISSION OF THE CHURCH

Once again, whenever one hears talk of "mission" in the church today—such as "that church is not on mission," or "we need to be on mission," it seems that what most people mean by it is the sort of engagement with the world that one might associate with "redemption" and "restoration"; in short, they mean "missions," or God's plan and purpose to engage the lost world. But as we have already seen, this cannot be indicative of God's larger purpose. What I propose, then, is a shift away from "missional" talk or thinking, at least to the degree that it is sometimes emphasized today. Let me once again make it plain, lest I be misunderstood. I am not in any sense claiming that God is not "missional," as we will see in a moment; nor am I claiming that a central part of God's overall mission is not the redemption of his elect and the restoration of his creation. I am simply arguing that any understanding of the "mission" of God that seeks to be an organizing or centering notion, but which fails to take into account God's larger purpose in the world, fails likewise to do justice to the God of the Bible. God's ultimate purpose is to glorify himself, or to make himself preeminent and to make his greatness known, in every aspect of life. To be "on mission" in an ultimate sense, then, is to align ourselves with the will of God in every area of life, and to seek his will and honor in each of those areas. There are certainly priorities, to be sure; and "missions" is clearly one of these for the church today, a foundational and primary one. But as we shall see, even missions must be subservient to God's ultimate purpose. For in order to glorify God, missions must be undertaken in God's way, or according to God's will.

My wife and I had to learn some hard lessons after leaving the field. We were raised with a balanced perspective on the purposes of God, and knew that missions had to be done God's way, in God's timing, but it was still hard to abandon what seemed to us an incredibly urgent task. What we have had to do in the States is some hard thinking and some serious readjusting. The upshot of it is that even though we are firmly convinced of the priority of missions, and remain greatly burdened for the lost and dying of the world, we have become equally burdened that missions be done properly. In other words, God's glory in the person going, and in the methodology employed, is of no less importance to God than the outcome. They are each the "mission" of God, if you will. Furthermore, God will accomplish his purposes in redemption in his way, and with the laborers he chooses. These claims might seem unsettling to some, but I trust after some consideration they will make biblical sense.

First though, we need to make a bit more clear exactly what it is the church is to do. To begin, surely every Christian must understand that we now live in a special age, an age that must be considered normative. It is, as theologians commonly refer to it, the age (or era) of the church. I think these things are fairly obvious in the New Testament. The apostolic writings make it clear that it was God's intention, after the resurrection of Jesus, for new, Spirit-filled believers to gather in local churches, which together make up the church universal, or the body of Christ. And this church, indeed, does have a mission, including a mission in the world: as 1 Peter 2:9 makes clear, we are to "proclaim the excellencies" of him who called us. We are, indeed, to seek to be "lights in the world," as Philippians 2:15 instructs us. This, I take it, is essentially a continuation of what Christ calls all his followers to do. Thus, certainly, we must establish and make absolutely clear that the church is, at its foundation, those who continue in obedient discipleship as Jesus commanded. Whatever the church is to do, it cannot stray too far from this foundational calling. And to be a disciple of Jesus, clearly, means to engage the world with the gospel and with acts of love and charity. "Missions," then, however we define it, is an essential calling of the church. For it continues the "mission" of Christ, if one wishes to speak of mission. We will touch on this more in a moment.

But what seems to be missing in many churches today, frankly, especially some in broadly Evangelical circles—and it seems Southern Baptists are particularly culpable here—is a full and proper understanding of the other great purpose, or purposes, that the church is called to. These, I would argue, are the church's *internal* duties, for lack of a better term. One great legacy of the Reformation, and in particular the English Puritans of the 17th century, is a proper understanding of, and emphasis on, the way God's church is to be conducted. Our Lord, it turns out, is vitally concerned about how affairs in his church are to be carried out, as passages such as 1 Timothy 3:15 make clear. It is, after all, the "household of God, which is the church of the living God, the pillar and support of the truth." The universal church, expressed in various locations, is the very body of Christ, but also the habitation of God himself, which will be finally and fully consummated in eternity. Therefore, conduct in God's house is incredibly important to Him. Among other things, there should be no immorality in it, and it should conduct its own internal enforcement of God's standards (1 Cor 5:10–13); it must be about certain duties, such as prayer (1 Tim 2:1 and following); it must choose certain qualified leaders (1 Tim 3:1 and following); it must have services of worship and praise to God, in which a variety of soul-building exercises take place; and on we could go.

Those in the Reformed tradition sought to recapture the importance of these things, though one could certainly argue that they went a bit far. In fact, having been raised in such a context myself, one in which old Puritan confessions like the London Baptist Confession of 1689 were held to rather dogmatically, I can say that balance was rarely achieved. There was, indeed, a modern Reformation movement of sorts in the United States from the late 1960s on, and it was initially a good thing. American Evangelicalism had resorted to extremely low levels of seriousness in general; God's love and the so-called "easy-believism" movement were in full swing. Superficiality in all things biblical reigned; cultural Christianity, especially in the South, was in its heyday. Interestingly, the one thing that remained steadfast in these churches was an emphasis on reaching the lost, albeit with a less-than-biblical presentation of the gospel. And, as an aside, I am not entirely sure the situation is much different in the Southern Baptist world today. Reformed doctrine has made an obvious comeback over the past fifty years or so, to be sure, even in the Southern Baptist Convention, but in the Southern Baptist churches I have attended, doctrine still seems to be of secondary importance. Indeed, one's greatest achievement in the Christian life is said to be "witnessing," and members are constantly rebuked for not engaging the lost. Not even Christlike character overshadows this pinnacle of Christian living, despite Paul's warnings about such misguided emphasis in such passages as 1 Corinthians 13.

But as I say, the Reformed movement sought to correct these things, and did so. However, again, perhaps they went too far. For many Reformed Baptist churches either neglected the Great Commission altogether or spoke of it only half-heartedly. Indeed, there are a host of issues connected to these matters, doctrinal and otherwise. Suffice it to say here, what is needed in all things is balance. What the Reformed community needs to recapture, to be sure, is an emphasis on the mission of Christ in all its aspects, including its emphasis on engaging the lost world. But what the larger Evangelical community needs to recapture in my view, even the larger community that claims Reformed doctrine, is a re-centering on the doctrine of the glory of God in all things. There is a proper way for the church to conduct itself internally; and there is a proper way for the church to conduct itself toward the world, or as it engages in missions. How to determine this method requires a careful handling of the biblical record. And so, in what follows, I wish to attempt to set forth a brief but hopefully biblically-faithful understanding of a few principles that should guide the church in its involvement with missions, with a special eye toward areas in which the modern Evangelical church may be failing.

AFFIRMING THE GREAT COMMISSION

Again, it is, without question, an essential calling of the church to continue to carry out the Great Commission. I say essential calling, because there is a curious lack of emphasis on such language in the pastoral epistles. And here we must proceed with care. All followers of Jesus must engage in his work, his mission. I will discuss in more detail what I believe this mission to be in a moment, but for now, I think it impossible to conclude otherwise than to argue for this foundational reality. As we have said, we are called to be disciples of Christ, and we are called to make disciples. A foundational duty of a disciple is to seek to make other disciples. This bit of Bible-based reasoning is, I think, unassailable, even if we bring in the multi-faceted duties and responsibilities incumbent upon all believers in the church age. To not engage in this work, then—to ignore the Great Commission—commits one to a theological position regarding the teaching of Christ that is untenable. We cannot ignore what he taught and what he did; quite the opposite, in fact. Thus, though we believe the writings of the later apostles to be inspired Scripture, of course, we cannot in any way pit them against the teachings of Jesus; the teachings of our Lord must be in some sense foundational, as we have said previously.

Balance is absolutely essential here, but I have said, balance is rarely achieved. The Reformed community, perhaps, too rarely emphasizes the life and ministry of Christ in the gospels, while the broader Evangelical community too rarely emphasizes the epistles. But surely balance can be had. And I believe it is imperative to establish that the call to discipleship that went out from our Lord, and his final command to go into all the world and make further disciples, and his teaching that the Holy Spirit would be sent out to help accomplish this task, and even the fact that the apostles themselves, in writing to the church, were engaged in this very task, all point to the primacy of Great Commission thinking. There is, after all, a mission of the church, that is subservient to the larger purpose of God in the world, and is certainly temporal, belonging uniquely to the church age; but it is a mission nonetheless. And it is to carry on the work of Jesus, until the end of time. We must, then, be "on mission" in this sense.

The curious lack of emphasis on the Great Commission in the epistles, however, as I have said, warrants some consideration. As we have already seen, the apostles had the mission of Jesus in view for all believers, as they express in key verses. But there is a noticeable lack of emphasis on "witnessing," to use the common term, across the range of the later New Testament. At the very least, it is not emphasized nearly as much as it usually is in Evangelical churches today, especially Baptist churches. In fact, without going into a full-fledged discussion of it, the pattern that emerges from Paul especially is that the participation in evangelism that the church should engage in is primarily support of "front-line" ministers such as Paul himself. It is Paul who has been entrusted with the gospel to the Gentiles; the churches are asked by him to engage in prayer for his work (Eph 6:19–20, Col 4:3–6, 2 Thess 3:1–2, etc.). What, then, are we to make of this?

Here, too, as in our consideration of the time and context of our Lord and his call to discipleship, some consideration of the same in Paul will assist us. Paul, we must remind ourselves, did have a unique mission, as the last of the apostles (1 Cor 15:8). He was set apart by God for work among the Gentiles with full apostolic authority, and the epistles are written, in most cases, to churches he has founded or helped to found. There is, then, even a logical order to the work of missions that Paul is engaged in: sinners are called and saved, then "plugged into" the local church, where they begin to grow as church members, with all of their newfound duties and responsibilities. Some of the epistles, then, at least to some degree, represent that time or stage in the work of missions that involves the establishment, growth, and maturity of recent converts. Other epistles, to be sure, are written largely for other reasons, such as to address certain issues; but my point here is simply that it certainly makes sense that Paul the apostle would not write to his recent converts and expect them immediately to begin some sort of serious gospel ministry, especially along the lines of what he is doing. But does Paul's emphasis hold for us today? I am going to argue that there is at least one sense in which it does.

MINISTRY: A HIGH CALLING

The issue of apostleship has been much discussed and debated in recent years and remains controversial. Some, perhaps most, see apostleship as being limited to Paul and the original apostles, while others see there being more than twelve, with the possibility of so-called "little-a" apostles scattered throughout the New Testament, who likewise possess the full range of apostolic giftedness and authority. It seems to me that a definitive answer to this problem cannot be found in the Scriptures, except to say that the word "apostle" is certainly used to describe some that are clearly not part of the original group which included Paul, such as Barnabas in Acts 14:14, or Silvanus and Timothy, it seems, in 1 Thessalonians 6. Whether or not there are truly two categories of apostle in the New Testament, however, the use of the word apostle represents an interesting problem. Since the word apostle generally means "one sent on a mission," and since the New Testament meaning of the word clearly has that sense, when we consider the disciples becoming apostles, etc., the question may be raised whether anyone in the New Testament era could or would be sent on a missionary-type ministry without being considered an apostle in some sense. Of course, we recoil from this possibility with a heartfelt "no"; certainly one was not expected or required to be a full-fledged apostle in order to engage in the work of missions. Indeed, when the early church was scattered (Acts 8:4), everyone went about preaching the word. But I would argue that there is yet a difference between ordinary gospel witness, and gospel ministry. There is a sense, to be sure, in which gospel ministry is unique and special, and not, as we shall see, for all or young believers. And if this is the primary takeaway from our study of Paul's ministry and missions, it is indeed vital.

What I am arguing, then, in essence, is simply this: while the office of apostleship remains difficult to pin down and apply today, a principle we can certainly take away from Paul's discussion of his office, and indeed from a study of ministry in the Word of God at large, is an incredibly important, but all-too neglected principle: ministry, especially gospel ministry, is only for those who are "set apart," as Paul put it in Romans 1:1, for that purpose. It is clear in the Word of God, if one takes the time to study it out, that there is a crucial difference between our Lord's call to his twelve disciples and his call to everyone else—a difference not necessarily in *devotion*, but in *vocation*. There is a difference as well between those scattered by persecution who went about preaching the word, and the divinely-called and Spirit-appointed ministry of church planting engaged in by the Apostle Paul. The distance here is the same as that between pastor and pew. The difference is one of *ministry*, of being divinely prepared, divinely called, divinely gifted, and divinely empowered for a particular task in the kingdom of God. The fact of the matter is that the principal work of missions, biblically-speaking, is not to be carried out by *normal* or *all* Christians; it is to be carried out by those biblically called and prepared for such. "Set apart for me Barnabas and Saul," the Holy Spirit says in Acts 13:2, "for the work to which I have called them."

Certainly there are nuances here. Some may be called to the primary work of missions, which is concerned with preaching the gospel and planting churches, while others may justifiably be called, again following biblical principle and practice, to come alongside and help them, even for a short time, as John Mark helped Paul. And certainly all Christians are to be actively involved in evangelism wherever God has placed them. We don't want to so guard such things, as many in Reformed circles are prone to do, that much of the good that could be done in a variety of missions-related settings is lost. What I am contending is simply this: the work of missions, properly understood, is a God-appointed ministry set aside for those prepared, called, anointed, and then sanctioned and sent by the Spirit (and the church) for this purpose. And I humbly contend as well that the Evangelical church today seems to have an insufficient understanding of the significance of these things.

Going back to the Old Testament, we see God preparing Moses (for 40 years!) in the wilderness, and then we see the call, the anointing, and the mission carried out. The experience of Paul in the New Testament mirrors this process exactly. So does the experience of the twelve themselves, of course. This idea of *preparation* clearly involves gaining maturity, or sanctification, and experience. I now believe that my father's first ministry opportunity, for example, which involved 20 years in pastoral ministry, was nothing other than preparation for his real calling, the work of training other pastors in foreign countries.

The *call* of God to ministry is as prominent in the New Testament as that of preparation. It is often shrouded in mythical speculation, but for many does not come via a burning bush, but rather a quiet burning of soul. But note the importance of the verification of one's call in the biblical record; there is a testing (1 Timothy 3:10) and a careful consideration (1 Timothy 5:22) involved in all matters of ministry. And then there is the *anointing* or empowerment, which comes through the laying on of hands—now largely a symbolic gesture, but then a literal conveying of power. The Holy Spirit in the days of the early church was indeed passed from an anointed person to one not so anointed, and even many today take 1 Timothy 4:14, in which Timothy's spiritual gift is bestowed by the elders, as normative. What emerges from these things is as simple as it is easy to abuse. There are those who are called to special ministries in the service of God, and these must be prepared by God, called, anointed, and sent. In all of these processes, the work of God the Holy Spirit is primary, but all is done through the agency of God's appointed leaders and his church.

It is important to note that these are not first and foremost *technical* matters, but *spiritual* ones. God is not going to anoint someone who is not prepared by Him. It is, again, *his* work. Much of this simply goes back to the notion of holiness. God's preparation is designed to make men holy. There is, of necessity, a period of time that must take place to achieve any real degree of holiness in this life, and God delights in the process. He doesn't shortchange or hasten it; he is glorified in every slow, minute, painstaking detail of it! And his Holy Spirit will not fall on those who are not so purified, so prepared. Just as the prayers of righteous people are those used by God, so their deeds. We should look at it this way: the work of God in our souls is his slow possession of us by his Holy Spirit, bit by bit. And to the modern Evangelical world, I say: to the degree that this is rushed or taken lightly, to that degree a prospective pastor or missionary is virtually guaranteed to be without the power of Almighty God. There may be some exceptions, but we need desperately to recover this sense of patience in God's preparation of his workers, both in the church in general, but especially in missions, where such a perspective seems desperately lacking.

GLORIFYING GOD IN THE SENDING PROCESS

In my twenty-plus years of missions experience, on the field and in the States, working with sent teams overseas and sending and training teams here, it is my honest belief that missions in the Evangelical world, much like the church, is in a state of spiritual dilapidation. Much of the problem can be traced back to the sending process. And though it pains me to say it, I cannot help but think it undeniable that "necessary evils" such as seminaries and sending agencies are part of the problem. There is no question that these have done some harm as well as good, though I would be hesitant to assign too much blame to the institutions themselves. They are, in a very real sense, necessary, for a variety of practical reasons. And they have done much to facilitate the work of missions around the world in the modern period, as every student of Christian history knows. But the genuine Christian must always recalibrate himself upon the word of God. And the sober reality from the Word of God is this: the sincere men (and women) in the vast ranks and levels of leadership in seminaries and especially sending agencies are, quite simply, unqualified to serve in ministry leadership roles by very definition. In the church of God, there is no authority outside of God-appointed elders, unless one wishes to claim apostolic authority. Elders are, like missionaries, divinely-called and anointed for their work, and they are responsible for overseeing ministries. These are the ones God has appointed to shepherd and guide the flock, and, again, in the absence of apostolic (or if one wishes, prophetic) authority, these are the only authorities in the church that the Word of God recognizes. The point here is that spiritual decisions, such as those involved in the sending forth of missionaries, simply should not be done by "para-church" organizations and leaders. There is no such thing as an independently operated para-church organization in the Bible; there is only the church of God! So right here at the foundation of missions, we have a huge problem, especially in western countries: a large part of the decision-making process in missions has been taken over by agencies populated by men and women who are not occupying biblically-sanctioned roles. Again, let us make no mistake about it: this is not a technical issue, it is a spiritual one. And it all points directly back to the centrality of God in all things. There is a reason why God has set things up this way in his church, and in his operations. It is so that he would be supreme in all things; so that his power would gain the victory.

Again, the danger here is that there is a lack of spirituality in the whole process today, and it relates not only to those being sent but to those doing the sending. This matter of divine preparation, call, and anointing are not by-the-way matters; they are the very lifeblood, so to speak, of how God works—because *they are God working*. And so I would claim the following about the sending process: to the degree that any system, organization, or so-called ministry leader is usurping the appointed process of almighty God, and the rightful place of God's elders and church in the sending process, to that degree the work they are doing is not only misguided, but ripe for failure. And to the degree that a prospective missionary is "rubber-stamped" by an agency or a seminary upon the mere completion of a program, to that degree the endeavor is likely to fail. Not that almighty God cannot and does not use even misguided means; of course he does. But in this the Reformed community got it right: there is a way things are to be done, a way that glorifies God. And that way is for divinely-placed elders to carefully consider the seriousness of the call to gospel ministry, and to carefully and deliberately screen all those who put themselves forward for such ministry.

A deeper problem, of course, is the state of the church itself, and in particular its pastors. I have seen so many young and undeniably immature pastors in American churches since I have returned! Particularly in large Southern Baptist churches. Pastors who, frankly, have no business shepherding others, much less taking on the title of "elder." Those called to the pastorate must not only be approved and blameless, but must not be new converts (1 Timothy 3:6). And neither can Timothy's youthfulness be used as a counter-example; biblical historians place him at least around thirty years old, which is, bizarrely, veteran status in many Southern Baptist churches! Indeed, this is one very serious critique I have of the mega-church or rapidly-multiplying church movement that is so in vogue today: the work of shepherding is being cast to the side. Young, recently-graduated, and thoroughly unproven pastors are often thrust into leadership roles in such churches, roles for which they are patently unqualified, all because of exponential church growth—or because they have been groomed to be loyal to the church brand. But there is no mistaking it: shepherding simply cannot be done by young converts. So many today are being rushed into leadership roles unprepared! It truly is incredible. I add this side note: the seminary system, which once was populated by men who took the spiritual side of their job most seriously, is now being taken over by mere academics, if "academic" is even an appropriate title for the superficial scholarship that occurs in most Evangelical circles. And aspirants to the pastorate, much like prospective missionaries, are often deemed fit for the ministry simply by passing through such seminary ranks, with perhaps one or two years of a practical assistantship or internship added on. Academic knowledge, it seems, somehow equates to spiritual readiness today. But this cannot be.

All of this inevitably impacts missions. If the senders are immature, unprepared, and unfit, then how can they recognize potential laborers for missions? Indeed, the mission field is chock-full of virtually anyone and everyone who is willing to go (and there are plenty, it turns out). Young, single men, who (like myself decades ago) have no business engaging in serious missions work; young, single women, who, like the men, are often restless and unprepared; businessmen with absolutely no spiritual qualifications of any sort; eccentrics, more at home in a strange and distant culture than their own; retirees; adventurers; loners; drifters; romantics; the ambitious; the unsettled; the mysteriously unattached; these are the multitudes populating our mission fields! Somehow they are making it through the filtering process. God have mercy upon us, sincere as many of these people are. The whole Evangelical missions system is closer to a spiritual mess than to anything else. Some, indeed, are attempting to do the process right, and in the end, again, the system is not to blame so much as the general lack of spirituality and biblical knowledge and fidelity that plagues Evangelicalism. The Reformed community, particularly Reformed Baptists, got much of this right in the past fifty years, but failed to wed this knowledge to any real missionary zeal. The larger Evangelical community has the zeal, but not the knowledge. God help us bring the two together!

HOPE FOR THE FUTURE

Is there any hope for change? It cannot be too late. The world of missions faces more challenges than ever, perhaps. Rising costs have forced agencies into considering shortcuts; thus the "business as mission" movement was born. Some mega-church pastors, eager for change, are attempting to start massive movements of college students giving themselves up for missions—at least for a couple of years. Indeed, the two-year missions internship in Southern Baptists circles seems almost mandatory—call it the "Mormon Model"—but what it is accomplishing is dubious indeed. It took me over two years on the mission field just to figure out where I was, let alone see a national completely ignorant of all things spiritual come to any sort of understanding of what I was talking about. And people of all ages and stages of the Christian life are now being encouraged to do whatever they do somewhere strategic for the kingdom. It would be inappropriate, surely, to pour cold water on all these well-meaning attempts; what needs to occur, in my opinion, is consistent and ongoing reformation. Those in places of leadership in our churches need to return to the Word of God and begin to take seriously the glory of God in the doing of missions, from start to finish. Their role is primary and of the utmost seriousness. God will not bless those he has not prepared, called, anointed, and properly sent. We dare not rush this process, no matter the needs of the world. And the church-planter—the properly-called and anointed man, a man of maturity, holiness, experience, wisdom, and spiritual power—is still the man to take the gospel into new places. And his calling is for all intents and purposes a permanent, lifelong one. The Bible makes this clear—but where is this idea in the Evangelical church today? There will always be room for others to come alongside and help this man of God; but these must know their place, and these must also be properly sent. The work of God, again, is just that—a work of his Holy Spirit. No one insufficiently anointed can usurp this work. God first sanctifies those he empowers. This process takes time. It truly is a special privilege to be "set apart" for ministry, and a high calling.

Again, all Christians, to be sure, are called to some ministry (1 Cor 12:5; Eph 4:12)—primarily, we should note, within the body of Christ. And all Christians, we have already established, are to be involved in gospel ministry in some capacity; first and foremost through the means of prayer. How foundational the work of prayer is to the task of missions! From what we have already seen, I believe we can safely infer that the vast majority of saints are to engage in prayer for the few who are called specifically to the work of missions. Intercession, once again, is the church's primary duty.

Again, one should not seek to draw doctrines out of personal experience, but in my case it was clear. God is not interested first in what I do, for missions or otherwise; he is interested in *who I am becoming* (yet another pearl of wisdom from the ministry of my father). It is this that gives him glory above all. And he is glorified by using people the way he wants; and the result is often humbling. Indeed, how *utterly* humbling are the ways of God! When I went overseas, I thought I was being a true disciple of Jesus. I was following him as I should. Shouldn't everyone, I thought, be a missionary? Aren't all Christians automatically missionaries, as is commonly taught? The answer to this, again, is yes and no. *Yes* if you mean that all Christians are to engage the lost and needy world where God has placed them—with the gospel and, as we will see in a later chapter, with acts of love and kindness. *No* if you mean missionaries in the full and proper sense of the term. Evangelicalism dare not blur these boundaries, as so many are eager to do, because the Word of God does not blur them.

God raises up his own servants to do his work, those whom he has divinely prepared or matured, called, and anointed by the Spirit of God. Only such men and women can know God's power and blessing in their ministry, for only such people are people *of God*. May God raise such up again in our day!

5

Idols

My mother's father, John McKeithen, was of Scotch-Irish descent, born to humble and decent people in a rural parish in northwestern Louisiana. They were Christians, but whether they were real ones, and not merely the cultural kind, was hard to say. In truth, though, serious Christianity goes pretty far back on my grandfather's side, and various legendary family stories passed down attest to the fact. Several generations back, the family boasted a pistol-packing, female Methodist circuit rider; and my grandfather's own grandmother, Granny Jane, was apparently very vocal in church services, never afraid to call down relatives in the middle of worship who weren't praising God in a manner she thought fitting. Of course, what always seemed to shine through the most in these stories, rivaling and often overshadowing the religious zeal, was the infamous McKeithen personality, that odd and often inscrutable mixture of fragile sensitivity and bombastic, overpowering temper—a genetic legacy that, in the end, none of us could entirely escape. I referenced it before in the story of my mother, but my grandfather had it in spades, and without, sad to say, the softening effects of grace. I can still hear his booming voice echoing down the long corridor of his final home, a one-story, seemingly never-ending mansion on the grounds of an old Louisiana plantation. Cotton was still farmed there, and wildlife were plenteous. As soon as we arrived for visits, my grandfather would inevitably pile us into the family jeep, a staple in his constantly-updated fleet of American-made cars, and ride us around his vast property like a demagogue, surveying the blooming crop rows that filed past like an army summoned in endless, orderly ranks for review. His voice boomed everywhere we went; I wondered if it did so before he was famous.

But that's no matter, for famous he became. He survived the Second World War and came home to start his life the possessor of multiple medals for bravery and an insatiable hunger to make something of himself. Having earned his law degree and gotten married before his years of military service, he began his law practice humbly and worked his way to undeniable success, making a living in the early days by representing the poor and disenfranchised. He soon became interested in politics, befriending and ultimately becoming a successor of sorts to Earl Long, one half of the infamous political duo that both wrecked and resurrected depression-era Louisiana. However that whole misty relationship unfolded, the results were clear and stunning; my grandfather eventually wound up as governor of Louisiana in 1964, winning a narrow victory by marshaling the vote of the same disenfranchised citizens he had worked so long and hard to represent.

There had to be some authentic goodness in him, it would seem; he could cause division, and most of the time it seemed people either loved or hated him, but in those who loved him he inspired a fierce and abiding loyalty that both surprised and ultimately saddened me. His legacy as Louisiana governor remains clear, if not pure; there have even been those who insist that he could have made it onto the national political scene, and what a president he would have made. Whether the former is true or not is, of course, speculation, but the latter claim seems not to have been. Like so many great political leaders, he was a man of undeniable talents; he had razor-sharp intuition, an almost x-ray-like ability to read people's motives and deconstruct their intentions, a talent that could be imposing and unsettling at times; he possessed courage and a tireless work ethic; and most importantly of all, he did maintain some genuine moral sense, and held himself to a sufficient ethical standard to be admired by many of the salt of the earth-type people who elected him again in 1968. It may have been, indeed, this moral standard, this lack of internal corruption, that ultimately led to the dismantling of his political career, but that is not our story.

Whatever my grandfather's personal moral standard, it did not extend to the level of genuine Christianity. Somewhere along the line my grandfather abandoned the faith he was raised to believe and follow. By the time I knew him, he was incessantly bursting into gospel song and talking about his daily good deeds to whomever would listen, but privately, my mother told me, he was resisting her every effort to repent, and claiming the need to see "one more miracle" from Jesus. His ambition kept him busy, but like many men of his generation, his most telling legacy may have been his inability to sincerely connect with his family. He favored those children (and grandchildren) who could make worldly successes of themselves, who had the inclination to gain and hold the spotlight, and he was incapable of deep affection toward those family members who didn't, I thought. Though he certainly respected my parents for their beliefs, he occasionally goaded them about their apparent earthly failures, tempting them with offers of financial assistance, if only they would try to get themselves more directly into the public eye. He was, for all intents and purposes, the *world* to us, a world we had long ago rejected. He died in 1999, when I was freshly graduated from college and thirty thousand feet above the earth, headed east, as far away from that world as one could get.

Fast forward ten years later. Sure, I had lived through the rise of the Religious Right in the eighties, but nothing had prepared me for the conservative political fervor I was about to experience in the Christian school in which I now worked. Here I was, a veteran of nearly a decade of work in a country where political opposition meant prison and even death, in which I had tried to witness for the gospel—knowing, of course, that the one thing more dangerous than discussing religion was discussing politics—and I was finding that the situation in American Christian schools was virtually the same. Only this time, the danger lay in questioning not communism, but the twin demigods of capitalism and freedom.

Growing up, the situation had been clear. There was the kingdom of this world, with its emphasis on earthly greatness and power—epitomized by my grandfather—and the kingdom of Christ, which turned every worldly notion of greatness on its head. One focused on the affairs of this world, the other the affairs of heaven. It was simplistic, to be sure, but after years of study and reflection on the issue—I'm not so sure it *was* simplistic. But here in this Christian school, even the mere questioning of the biblical support for notions like capitalism and freedom, or the questioning of the degree to which Christians should be involved in earthly affairs, labeled me a pariah. Even more bizarre, the terms "liberal," "socialist," and even "communist" began to be thrown around about my supposed views, even though no one had ever asked me about them or engaged me in conversation. What I was uncovering is that in the Evangelical Christian community there is a set of closely-held convictions on the above topics, and attempts to challenge these beliefs are often met with hostile opposition. I have now come to believe that other than physical pleasure or earthly security, there is perhaps no greater idol in the American church today than what I will call for the sake of convenience "politics." And I am equally convinced that if the church does not rid itself of this idol, there is absolutely no hope for a movement of the Spirit of God among his people.

POLITICS IN THE CHURCH: THE PROBLEM

As with most of the topics we have broached in this book, this issue is obviously bigger than one chapter allows, and many useful books have come out of late on just this issue of questioning the church's interest and involvement in political affairs. Nevertheless, I am sufficiently burdened to proceed, and to add my own experience and concerns to the (thankfully) growing trend of troubled voices. As I have already mentioned, I have spent time in many contexts where the majority of professing Christians had little to no real understanding, in my view, of New Testament teaching on the kingdom of heaven, and how it contrasts with earthly kingdoms and involvement with them. Indeed, there are few matters to speak of that have not been more covered over in confusion, misapplication of biblical texts, and the like. I am going to contend in this chapter that the matter is actually much simpler than it often appears, and hopefully my brief but I trust useful comments will help us some gain some clarity on the issue. Whether or not hearts will be changed, however, is another matter altogether, and one over which I can do little but pray.

First of all, what, then, is the problem with politics and the American church? Put quite simply, political interest and involvement have become, in my view, an *idol*, and one that is perhaps as deeply held as any, excluding, as I have said, purely physical desires or desires for security. Going back to our model of the importance and primacy of the passions, Christians inevitably talk about politics when they are together, get angry when discussing it—far more passionately so, often, than when discussing any spiritual thing—and have concocted a wide variety of defenses of their favorite convictions. They tend to band together and form friendships based on political convictions, and those who differ are often unfairly categorized, labeled, and avoided. Clearly, political issues, for many Christians, touch on things that are at the core of either their identities as human beings or their most deeply-held beliefs.

It would seem here that I am describing a select group of people in the world; sadly, however, as we all can testify if we are being honest, this description rather aptly fits a fairly large group of people in the Evangelical church. Things seem to have gotten worse in the past few years, and now politics is as divisive and distracting as ever within the body of Christ. Christians are avoiding meaningful fellowship with each other, leaving churches to join new ones, and are just as vocal and often unkind in their criticisms of each other as people in the world. The result is an Evangelical church that is threatening to fracture over various political issues; and no amount of reasoning seems able to budge certain Christians from their convictions.

There is an immediate temptation to dismiss such people as either hopelessly unspiritual, thoroughly unintellectual, or both. But of course we can't. The Bible calls us to unity in the strongest possible terms. Furthermore, these issues have been explored by various influential theologians over the past two centuries, and the ideas of some of these thinkers continue to have real influence. What we must do, then, with all patience, is continue to lovingly seek to engage our brothers and sisters in conversation, open the pages of the Word of God, and try to ascertain what, in the end, our true purpose and mission should be, and rally around it.

TWO INFLUENCES

When one begins to explore this matter even a little bit, one finds two figures who divide the lion's share of influence among those in the church who are passionate about politics: Abraham Kuyper, a Dutch theologian and statesmen from around the turn of the twentieth century, and H. Richard Niebuhr, an American theologian from the early-to-mid twentieth century or so. Indeed, it is rather commonplace in theological circles to identify the emergence of the branch of Reformed thought known as Dutch Calvinism with Kuyper and his generation of thinkers; one of the key differences between this new stream of Calvinistic thinking and older ones is just this issue of political involvement and cultural engagement. And the influence of Niebuhr can hardly be overstated. Thus, in order to deal with this issue with any degree of competency at all, one must at least touch on the beliefs of these two theologians and see how in the world this shift in thinking has taken place.

Astonishingly—or rather, not so astonishingly, I suppose, when one considers the deplorable intellectual state of Evangelicalism—much of Kuyper's influence can be traced to a single quote, given in his speech at the opening of the Free University of Amsterdam in 1880: "There's not a square inch in the whole domain of human existence over which Christ, who is Lord over *all*, does not exclaim, 'Mine'!"[1] In the popular Christian world, this has been interpreted as meaning, in line with Kuyper's own thinking, that since Christ has Lordship over every area of life and culture, we should "take culture back" for Christ, or seek to establish his Lordship in all areas. For the sake of this discussion, we can call this the "dominion" view.[2] Now, if cultural dominion were indeed the church's duty, this would, without question, cause a massive shift in focus and priority for the individual Christian and the church as a whole. If it is part of every Christian's task to claim cultural spheres for Jesus, such as education, the arts, and the political sphere, then the implications for Christian behavior would be massive and far-reaching. And so they have been among those who think this way. What we have seen in the past 50 or so years within Evangelicalism is an undeniably powerful trend toward cultural involvement. This way of thinking seems most at home among Presbyterians, but the Reformed leanings of such thinkers as Kuyper have seemed to give this way of thinking fluidity among any who claim a Calvinistic doctrinal heritage. And of course it finds a home easily among the broader Evangelical community, who is all too ready, I have suggested, to be at home in the world.

To all of this I say unequivocally and without apology: may such corruption of Christ's kingdom and mission vanish instantly and forever from the thinking and practice of the church! How dare the purity and simplicity of Christ and his mission be taken over by worldly-minded, divided forces, acting supposedly in the interest of our Lord. And neither are these issues subtle or difficult, as some theologians claim. I contend without any qualms at all that Jesus is not in any sense interested in taking over cultural spheres, or any aspect of this present world. To claim otherwise would mean that our Lord has *ambitions* for such things; that

---

1. Kuyper, "Sphere Sovereignty," as quoted in Carson, *Christ and Culture*, 214.

2. I use this term in a broad sense and merely for convenience here; in no way do I mean to associate Kuyper's views with Dominion Theology or Dominionism, though there is clearly some overlap.

he has desires and designs to be recognized as Lord over the arenas of this world. How far this is from the clear testimony of our Lord's life and words in the Scriptural record! Our Lord said clearly that "my kingdom is not of this world" (John 18:36). Furthermore, everything he did was for the spiritual and physical good of individual souls. He is a king, indeed, and he has come to establish his kingdom, but it is not of this realm. Christ's power and authority indeed have been fully inaugurated, but our Lord is not interested in ruling over the spheres of the here and now. In this present age, he is interested in ruling over his church and the hearts of men. His full and final rule over all will be established in the age to come. Again, the example of our Lord's life and ministry and the witness of the rest of the New Testament make this plain and undeniable.

D.A. Carson elucidates the fundamental confusion Evangelicals seem to be making here:

> Doubtless the passage from Kuyper most frequently quoted is this: "Oh, no single piece of our mental world is to be hermetically sealed off from the rest, and there is not a square inch in the whole domain of our human existence over which Christ, who is sovereign over all, does not cry, 'Mine!'" Yet that truth, which all thoughtful Christians will confess, must be integrated with other truths—for example, that Christ's sovereignty is widely contested now as it will not be in the new heaven and the new earth; that until the end an unavoidable tension exists between the covenant community of God's people and those who, on Christian terms, do not know him; that there is an epistemological chasm between those who accept God's revelation in Jesus Christ and those who do not.[3]

In other words, says Carson, Jesus does indeed reign over the entire universe, including earth—and we should add, he always has and always will—in the sense that he has supreme authority and power, and does whatsoever he wishes. But clearly he is not directly reigning over the earth and its cultural spheres in the here and now, as their acknowledged ruler. His sovereignty on the earth is, as Carson says, contested at best, and most often completely dismissed, of course. But there is much more here: the Bible speaks clearly of the fact that it is Satan who has been given temporary rule over the domain and affairs of men. Paul even calls him the "god of this world" (2 Cor 4:4), a claim Satan himself makes to Jesus (Luke 4:6). Pressing further, we see a clear contrast in the New

---

3. Carson, *Christ and Culture*, 214.

Testament between this world, or age, and God's kingdom in the age to come. Let us recall that we are not to be conformed to this world (Rom 12:2) or seek its wisdom (1 Corinthians 3:19). We are not to seek the riches of this present world (1 Tim 6:17); it is the poor of this world who will inherit the riches of Christ's kingdom (Jas 2:5). And we are to avoid loving the world and the things in in, for it is passing away (1 John 2: 15–17). Indeed, says John, it is the "last hour" of this present age; and Paul confirms that the wisdom and rulers of this age are passing away (1 Cor 2:6). How absurd, then, with all the biblical contrasts between this present world and age, and Christ's kingdom and the age to come, that any Christian would even begin to think that our Lord Jesus is interested in "ruling" over the spheres of the present culture! I do not think the meaning of his statement in John 18, that his kingdom is not of this world, can be any clearer, a statement which was fully backed up by his own refusal to assert his authority on earth, and his purpose instead to be crucified for the redemption of his people. It is clear in Scripture: our Lord is not interested in earthly power, realms, spheres of culture, etc. His reign has indeed been announced and inaugurated in the coming of the kingdom of heaven, but for now he is content to reign in the hearts of men and in his church. It is the church, then, and not the spheres of the world, that Christ is actively ruling over; and it is in the church that we see his ultimate, finale rule foreshadowed.

And indeed all disciples of Jesus are called to the same mindset. The entire rest of the New Testament, beginning with the book of Acts, is a clear and undeniable picture of Christ's followers imitating him—being devoted to spreading his light and love in the world, and then banding together as churches to in some sense preview the age to come: worshipping God, building each other up, praying for all the saints, and also praying for the success of God's gospel in the world. I contend right off the bat, then, that to argue that Christ and his followers are to be interested in the cultural spheres of this present age is not only unsupported in the New Testament by any evidence whatsoever, it is clearly overturned by the overwhelming evidence to the contrary. Only a few theological notions are even available for those who claim differently to make use of, but they are inevitably twisted and taken to mean things that Jesus never intended, as the notion of Christ's reign has. To be distracted with the cultural spheres of this passing age smacks of worldliness, plain and simple. The notion that we are deliberately to attempt to take over the spheres of culture is simply wrong. Worse, it is likely a dangerous ploy of Satan.[4]

But we must press deeper. Perhaps no one has had more influence on this trend in Evangelicalism than H. Richard Niebuhr, whose book *Christ and Culture* continues to be used in support of similar thinking. Interestingly, however, Niebuhr's work has been shown, even definitively so, to be seriously lacking. Perhaps no work has shown this more powerfully than the classic *Resident Aliens* by Stanley Hauerwas and William Willimon. Neither of these theologians are likely to be labeled as Evangelicals, and both subscribe to what one might call an uncommon view on the matter of political involvement, a view that is very much in line with the Anabaptists of old. But neither of these facts should cause us to downplay or ignore the clarity of their critique.

Briefly stated, Niebuhr claims that there are five positions available to the church in this whole matter of the relationship between Christ and culture: Christ against culture, Christ of culture, Christ above culture, Christ and culture in paradox, and Christ transforming culture. Without getting into a detailed analysis of the various positions, which have been undertaken by many, suffice it say here, Niebuhr opts for the last view, thus attempting to legitimize cultural involvement for Christians. We can call this, after Hauerwas and Willimon, the "transformist" view. But as these authors note in a classic passage, worth quoting at length:

> H. Richard Niebuhr, in his *Christ and Culture*, offered a typology for conceiving of our theological dilemma ... Despite the allegedly sociological nature of Niebuhr's book and its appearance as an objective description of the church and the world, it was not too difficult to discern which type of ecclesiology Niebuhr preferred: Christ Transforming Culture. Although Niebuhr put the liberals in the "Christ of Culture" camp, his own "Christ Transforming Culture" was the church that liberal, mainline, American Protestantism aspired to be. It neither capitulated to culture nor irresponsibly detached itself from the culture. The transformist church busied itself with making America a better place in which to live, transforming society into something of which Jesus might approve.

---

4. I am well aware that modern-day postmillennialists, Christian Reconstructionists, and other fringe groups would beg to differ with the preceding claims; but how they can get past the clear teaching and example of Christ and his apostles on this matter is hard to fathom, eschatological leanings notwithstanding.

> We have come to believe that few books have been a greater hindrance to an accurate assessment of our situation than *Christ and Culture*. Niebuhr rightly saw that our politics determines our theology. He was right that Christians cannot reject "culture." But his call to Christians to accept "culture" (where is this monolithic "culture" Niebuhr describes?) and politics in the name of the unity of God's creating and redeeming activity had the effect of endorsing a Constantinian social strategy. "Culture" became a blanket term to underwrite Christian involvement with the world without providing any discriminating modes for discerning how Christians should see the good or the bad in "culture." Niebuhr set up the argument in such a way as to ensure that the transformist approach would be viewed as the most worthy. A democracy like ours must believe that it is making progress, that the people are, through their own power and choice, transforming the world into something better than it would be without their power and choice. Thus Niebuhr set up the argument as if a world-affirming "church" or world-denying "sect" were our only options, as if these categories were a faithful depiction of some historical or sociological reality in the first place . . . There was a subtle repressiveness behind this seemingly innocuous pluralism. Niebuhr failed to describe the various historical or contemporary options for the church. He merely justified what was already there—a church that had ceased to ask the right questions as it went about congratulating itself for transforming the world, not noticing, that in fact the world had tamed the church.[5]

The authors' critique of Niebuhr here appears to include at least the following: (1) Niebuhr fails to adequately define or delineate what he means by "culture"; (2) he endorses a transformist approach without setting forth ways in which Christians are to first distinguish which aspects of culture to affirm or deny; (3) he sets up something of a false dilemma (world-denying sect vs. world-affirming church); and, perhaps most importantly, (4) he merely endorses what was already in full operation in the American church: the continuation of the task of, not the church, but the current democratic American culture, which was working to make society a better place on its own terms. In all of this, the authors conclude, Niebuhr clearly fails to establish the validity of the transformist position.

We do not have space to reevaluate Niebuhr in detail here, nor carefully analyze these two authors' treatment of him. Others have done so at

---

5. Hauerwas and Willimon, *Resident Aliens*, 39–42.

length, and the critique of Hauerwas and Willimon certainly stands on its own. For our purposes, the first point would take some time to trace out, time we don't have here, and while it is clear from even minor study on this issue that critiques two and three should be taken seriously, it is surely the last point that needs to be more carefully considered. First, however, let us consider evidence from other sources that Niebuhr fails to successfully establish his point of view.

We don't have far to look. On this matter Carson is again helpful, pointing out that in defense of his position, Niebuhr looks to John's gospel primarily, and to key voices in history; but, Carson notes, Niebuhr himself goes on to acknowledge that neither authority fully supports the transformist view! What Carson says here is again worth quoting:

> Niebuhr is a sufficiently careful reader of texts that even after he has milked the Fourth Gospel for all that he can take out of it—more in fact than is there—he finally concedes (as we have seen), "We are prevented from interpreting the Fourth Gospel as a wholly conversionist document, not only by its silence on many subjects but also by the fact that its universalistic note is accompanied by a particularistic tendency." Just so. But then one must ask whether the conversionist paradigm, at least in the ideal form in which Niebuhr wishes it would exist, is ever found in Scripture . . . Moreover, the greatest post-New Testament exemplars of this fifth pattern are, according to Niebuhr, Augustine and Calvin, until we arrive at F. D. Maurice. Augustine and Calvin are disappointing to Niebuhr because they do not follow the conversionist pattern all the way; F. D. Maurice turns out to be the hero, because he allows the conversionist pattern to take him into universalism—not on the ground that any New Testament document supports this line, but on the ground of what Maurice asserts he is "obliged" to believe in . . . Thus we are forced to wonder, by the same token, if Niebuhr's fifth pattern, at least in the pure form that Niebuhr prefers, has any real warrant for itself at all, save in the liberal theology of F. D. Maurice.[6]

According to Carson, then, what Niebuhr is left with in support of the transformist position is fairly thin; contradictory evidence (at best) in one book of the Bible, the gospel of John, and one scholar in history, a scholar who was undeniably liberal in his theology.

What Niebuhr is looking for, then, is simply not found in the New Testament. We have already challenged Kuyper's claim that Jesus wishes

6. Carson, *Christ and Culture*, 38.

to claim sovereignty in the cultural spheres of the here and now, and we would conclude with Hauerwas, Willimon, and Carson that Niebuhr's aims are similarly doomed. What is undergirding such thinking, clearly, are thoroughly unwarranted assumptions. When John uses world-affirming language, he is not attempting to argue for the transformation or redemption of culture; he is merely using symbolic language for the purpose of illustrating spiritual truths, as Carson notes.[7] To argue beyond this would clearly be going too far, especially in light of what the rest of the gospel of John makes plain. I would add that it would likewise be going beyond what the rest of the New Testament reveals of the clearly-stated intentions of Jesus and his followers, as we have already seen. Both the "dominion" view and the "transformist" view, then, are simply misguided, and badly so.[8] Again, what seems to be going on in both positions, I would argue, is an unwillingness to let go of the world entirely.

Thus it is here that Hauerwas and Willimon's fourth point starts to hit home. According to these two critics, what Niebuhr is actually doing is merely endorsing thinking that was already in the culture at the time. America was in the full flush of realizing what appeared for all the world to be the good and even necessary social changes occurring within its borders. Clearly, many Americans, even American Christians, were beginning to be seduced by the attractive glow of democracy, freedom, prosperity, and peace. Culture, it seemed, *was* being transformed, and that for the better. Surely Christianity had something to do with it! At the very least, it had to embrace it; it could not get in the way of what was clearly good.

What dangers are inherent in this way of thinking! The subtle draw of this "American" way of life is powerful indeed. Again, I fear that this, after all, is precisely what is behind the move toward cultural engagement and transformation in the church. As we will see in a moment, surely political involvement is not always wrong; furthermore, make no mistake about it: Jesus does have the power to transform culture! But this would be a secondary effect. Jesus is in the business of transforming human souls and building his church, and when enough of these souls are transformed by God's grace, then of course culture will be impacted as well.

---

7. Carson, *Christ and Culture*, 37.

8. I am aware that many, including Carson himself later in *Christ and Culture* and others such as Tim Keller in *Center Church*, seek to amend and recast these two views, but I have found the latter's work in particular to be unhelpful. Surely the matter of cultural involvement is not complex so long as the church's main purpose is kept in view.

And perhaps this indeed has occurred in various cultures in times past, though I believe the notion that this has happened in America needs to be far more carefully analyzed than it usually is.

Our Lord Jesus wants his church to pursue his mission of evangelism toward the lost, love and care for the needy, and sanctification within the church. We seek, above all else, to rescue human souls all around the world who are this very moment on the brink of eternity. Cultures come and go. There may indeed be wisdom in praying for and seeking to preserve certain aspects of a culture if they are more conducive to the gospel; indeed, Paul implores us to pray for all in authority, so that God's people might know peace (1 Timothy 2:1–2). But the preservation of that peace is not our primary or ultimate goal. Christ's disciples must be focused on his heavenly kingdom above all. And all we do must be for the sake of the mission of Christ.

When one considers certain cultural spheres in particular, such as the arts, one surely has at least some sympathy for the dominion or transformist view. Surely God, the very essence of beauty and the creator of the human capacity for art, wants us to pursue, enjoy, preserve, and redeem the arts! Or education, perhaps; surely Christ, in whom are hidden all the treasures of wisdom and knowledge, wants the truth about himself to reign supreme over all earthly educational institutions. And surely Christ, as Lord of all, wishes his reign to be acknowledged in earthly political spheres.

But these claims are not, I contend, ultimately biblical. The Jesus of the New Testament clearly does not wish to reign over earthly kingdoms, as we have seen. He is waiting to fully establish his own heavenly kingdom. And regarding the political sphere and even these other cultural spheres, while some might make these matters out to be hopelessly mired in theological complication, my contention is that this is not the case. How, then, might Christians think of cultural spheres and involvement in them in ways that are biblically faithful?

Take the arts—music, poetry, fiction, drama, painting, sculpting, and the like: God has obviously gifted us with the ability to do and to appreciate them. And the Bible even makes it clear that God intends Christians to engage in them, first of all in the praise of those things that are truly beautiful, beginning with God himself and all that he has made. Nearly the entire book of the Psalms firmly establishes the importance of praising God in music and poetry, to name two of the arts. But here, I contend, is how Christians should think of these things in light of the call of Christ to discipleship. (1) Provided they are in the service of what is true, beautiful, and good, these are things we should engage in and enjoy, both now and in eternity! It is breathtaking how figurative language pours from Jesus's lips even while fully committed to his Father's business. All the good things God has blessed the world with—the beauty of nature, the arts, etc.—are here to refresh and sustain us, even in our undeniably Christ-focused labors in the church age. (2) Nevertheless, until Christ's kingdom is fully consummated in the age to come, use and pursuit of these God-created, sinless enjoyments should be tempered, to focus more fully on the mission of Christ. Again, it is incredibly simple, really: nature, the arts, human relationships—all the good things God created—will be fully restored and returned to us *in the life to come*. For now, we are living in a unique age—an age between two kingdoms, as it were. The present age, originally created by God to be enjoyed but now tainted with sin, has been shown to be passing away; and the kingdom of heaven, when all things will be restored and also renewed or spiritually upgraded, so to speak—has been inaugurated, but not yet fully realized. This is the already-but-not-yet tension that theologians often speak of. There may be nothing sinful in using the Old World now, but we are called, earnestly by Jesus and his apostles, to live more and more in anticipation of the New. Significantly, this does not mean living as if the kingdom of heaven is already fully here; it means engaging in spiritual warfare to get more and more people into that heavenly kingdom. Then, at the end of the age, the unmitigated enjoyment of God and his things will commence in earnest.

It is undeniable that Christians have and will continue to struggle with Christ's demands. And the struggle over the arts is certainly a beautiful and worthy one. Tragically, I have known several sensitive souls who have turned away from following Christ on just this point—they believed his demand to focus on kingdom matters too challenging, particularly when it comes to the visual arts. But surely a proper theological understanding of the future state should encourage us *toward* Christianity, not lead us away from it! God is not going to destroy the arts; we are not headed, as Socrates would have us believe, toward a state devoid of all physical beauty! The Platonic "soul trapped in a body" view of human anthropology is surely wrong. The embodied soul is the ultimate human state, albeit with bodies recreated for the full and final indwelling of the Spirit of God, that we might enjoy God as never before. And surely all the beauty that God has given us to enjoy in this life will be experienced on a far grander scale throughout eternity, with the climax and indeed the substance of it all, of course, being enjoyment of our triune God himself.

Indeed, regarding the arts, would that more Christians would struggle with such issues! Sadly, however, this is not the case. Whether this is because the majority of Christians are merely enjoying the arts—or rather distorted, popular versions of the arts, without any tempering at all—or because the majority of Evangelicals are not truly interested in anything remotely artistic, is hard to say. What seems undeniable is that what occupies most Christians is not questions over the arts, but questions over *power*. I contend, once again, that what Hauerwas and Willimon imply is correct—Christians are obsessed with politics because what is at stake is one's way of life, a life dependent on freedom and economic prosperity. Indeed, to be precise, the great idol in this whole thing is perhaps not politics or even power in and of itself, but a way of life—the comforts and pleasures of a peaceful and prosperous earthly existence that certain political realities provide.

We have already established from the Word of God that neither politics nor any particular cultural sphere are things that matter to Jesus. But now we must turn to political involvement directly. Overemphasis on such is indeed, I fear to say, an idol that must be smashed into a thousand pieces and ground under our heels. Here, then, we had better seek to establish some biblical principles that can perhaps be, as it were, the first hammer blows.

KEY BIBLICAL PRINCIPLES ON POLITICS

Though there are many different aspects to this discussion, and in a sense it would be foolhardy to attempt to tackle this issue in a few pages, I do not believe the matter is overly complicated, as I stated previously. In fact, I believe that the matter becomes complicated only when one ignores the clear and obvious principles that the Word of God sets forth. Thus, I will at least seek to list those here, and hope that they are enough to make at least some headway on this contentious topic.

1. We have already stated and defended it, but it needs to be more fully examined: *Jesus and his followers were not interested in earthly power.* Our Lord made this absolutely clear on earth, as we have already seen. His mission is simple: to make disciples of all nations. These baptized disciples are to band together into churches that work to

build each other up, while also continuing the mission of Jesus in the world. This mission, to be absolutely clear, involves both sharing the gospel and also doing good to those in need, as Jesus did.

It is indeed a Christian truth, then, that church and state should in fact be separate—not because this truth was gradually developed in western countries through years of post-Reformation conflict or Enlightenment thinking, though no doubt it was—but because Jesus himself separated them. Jesus made it absolutely clear on earth, and the apostles later confirmed, that not only is the kingdom of heaven not of this world, and its citizens not to engage the authorities of this earth (John 18:36), but the church is to be its earthly picture, with its own authority and mission. As is widely known, it was in fact the Anabaptists—the little group who were often persecuted by the Reformers—who largely recovered this truth in the modern world, the Reformers being more inclined to keep church and state together during the early days of the Reformation. Certainly it seems the Reformers still had work to do in understanding the true nature of the coming of Christ's heavenly kingdom; indeed, perhaps many in the Reformed camp yet need to fully understand the discontinuity involved with its coming. But the point here is that it is not our business to run the affairs of this world. There is no question that the return of democratic processes to the western world in the last five hundred or so years has presented temptations to the church; the argument goes that much good for Christ can be accomplished through such political processes. But we will touch on this in a moment, under point three. For now, the boundaries are clear: we are Christians first and foremost. Our king is a heavenly king. Our kingdom is a heavenly kingdom, not of this age. Our mission is an eternal one, not a temporal one. Oh, how much good could be done in the American church if we could just recalibrate ourselves on this one point!

2. Flowing out of (1), *Christians are to be committed to loving Christ and living for his kingdom primarily and above all—or, perhaps better stated, with all their hearts.* As we have already seen, we are to aim for that zeal for God's house that Jesus had. In fact, it may be a truism, but it is one worth mentioning: to the degree that we have the Holy Spirit in our souls, to that degree we will be taken up with God's things. But God's things, again, are those things that Jesus was

taken up with, and those that the apostles, through the inspiration of the Holy Spirit, exhort us to. Jesus was consumed with zeal for the glory of God; the truth of God; the house of God; love for the lost; doing good to those in need; defeating Satan; prayer; etc. And we, as his followers, are to be of the same mind and heart, and on the same mission. Oh, the dangers of the delights of this present age! If Christians were really to get serious about the things Jesus is serious about, it is a legitimate question indeed what would remain of political interest and involvement. Precious little, no doubt.

Allow me a brief digression to drive this point home. In the New Testament, devotion to Christ and his things, the pursuit of holiness, etc., are presented as *all-encompassing, all-consuming things*. Consider Romans 12:1 and following, where we are told that we must, because of the mercies of God, present our bodies as a "living sacrifice" to God; and we are told that this is nothing other than our "rational service of worship." Note that the words "living sacrifice" echo the same call of our Lord Jesus to deny ourselves, take up our crosses, and follow him. Indeed, this imagery of crucifixion is repeated over and over again throughout the New Testament. We are told, for example, that true believers have "died with Christ" (Rom 6:8; Col 3:3), and have "crucified the flesh with its passions and desires" (Gal 5:24). We are, therefore, to consider ourselves "dead to sin, but alive to God" (Rom 6:11). But there is more. Not only are we to consider ourselves dead to sin, but we are henceforth to "walk in Him" (Col 2:6). We must not only put off our old selves, but we must put on the new (Eph 4:22ff), which is created after the very image of God (verse 24). It is imperative that we fully apprehend these principles! Because of our union with Christ in salvation, Christ is to be our *everything*, and we are to strive to work out his very image in our souls.

Another passage that expresses these sentiments is Philippians 3:7 and following, where the Apostle Paul expresses his desire to "count all things to be loss" in order to "gain Christ," and his desire to "press on toward the goal for the prize of the upward call of God in Christ Jesus." In these well-known verses, Paul is not saying that he is seeking salvation through his efforts, or that his salvation is yet uncertain; he is saying that he is behaving as though it is, and seeking to give his all to gain the prize, precisely because he has been "laid hold of" by Christ Jesus (verse 12)—that is, because Christ has saved him. His present knowledge of the true value of Christ, and his discovery of the way of salvation through him, have motivated him to give up everything for Christ, and he calls on all Christians to do the same (verse 15). And what is the scope or extent of his aims? That he would "know Him, and the power of his resurrection and the fellowship of his sufferings, being conformed to his death" (verse 10). So passionately in love with Christ was Paul, that he longed to live out our Lord's very life, even to the point of experiencing his same sufferings and death! This is beyond love; it is sanctified, Spirit-fueled obsession.

Does the church today know anything of what Paul is speaking of here? Do we understand the immensity of what he is giving up in order to truly know Christ—that is, "all things?" Can we not feel his grand earnestness, and the magnitude of the devotion he expresses? Then how are we obeying his exhortation? Are we accepting it and striving after it in our own lives, or are we rationalizing it away? Are we really "reaching forward," "pressing on," and "counting all things to be loss?" Do we really know what it means to live for this "one thing"?

Now we could multiply verses, but surely we need not belabor the point. The question we all need to ask ourselves daily—but especially when we consider this matter of political involvement, which has become, I contend, a genuine idol—is simply this: What can we point to in our lives that demonstrates any real degree of love and devotion to Christ and his things? Jesus was consumed with pleasing his heavenly Father and accomplishing his will on earth. And we are to follow in Christ's train by being just as fully committed to him. What things can we present as evidence in our lives of our commitment to the person and cause of Christ? And what in the world dare we hold back; what petty ambitions, desires, and joys should we even for a moment entertain, in light of the infinite blessings that are ours! For those who have been "blessed with every spiritual blessing in the heavenly places" (Ephesians 1:3ff), how can we do anything less than give God our all? For those of us who have reason to believe that we have been truly saved—given the gift of eternal life—how can this not be our one all-consuming ambition?

We Christians are called in these passages to put all of our effort and energy into this glorious task of loving God and sacrificing our lives for the cause of Christ. We should be spending great amounts of time, and making monumental efforts on a daily basis, and taking costly and even terrible pains, to live for Christ, both in our private lives and as his witnesses to a dying world. We should be doing all of this and more, so that we would be truly holy, and truly love Christ—as he calls us to—and do something for his kingdom and glory. And yet the bitter truth is this: most of us today who profess to be Christians are simply not putting forth this kind of effort. Our hearts do not beat for God and his things. We do not hunger and thirst for righteousness (Matt 5:6). We do not seek the kingdom of heaven and God's righteousness above all (Matt 6:33). It is not our "food and drink" to do the will of God and accomplish his work (John 4:34). We do not lament over the lost and perishing (Matt 23:37, Rom 10:1). And on we could go.

I would go so far as this, and here I will end this excursion: if our passion does not *mirror* or *reflect* the passion exemplified in the New Testament, in the example of Jesus and his apostles, and if our very goals, aims, and pursuits don't match what we see there, then what can we say about our aims and pursuits? How can we justify them? We cannot. Thus, I can state it boldly regarding politics: at the very least, if our interest and involvement in politics is not in the service of, or to accomplish the goals of, Christ and his kingdom, then it must be cast aside. Period. But this leads us to point three.

3. *Political involvement may be a good thing, especially when people's lives may be positively affected.* Here we are getting close to the heart of the issue. We have noted, of course, in what we have written previously, that the mission of Jesus involves making disciples of all nations, teaching them all that Jesus commanded. What Jesus commanded involves, necessarily, preaching the gospel, as is central in the work of the apostles; doing good to those in need, as he told us to time and again; planting and establishing God-honoring churches; and seeking to grow in holiness and sanctification. But in what way, then, or in what circumstances, might the issue of political involvement come into play? Potentially, many. I think the matter is quite simple; if there is good to be done to people, and the political means to accomplish it, then those political means should be utilized. Some more radical separatists among us might revolt against such thinking, but I think this principle may clearly be inferred from the work of Christ in the world, so I state it again: whatever means one might utilize to do good to others, as long as it is honoring to God and legally permissible, one should utilize, if God is so leading. The early Christians had no recourse to political power, as we all know. Neither have most Christians

throughout the ages. In our day, however, things have changed. And as history informs us, in the last several hundred years, great good has been accomplished for the needy and oppressed through the use of political means, in the very name of Jesus. One thinks of Wilberforce against slavery, a well-used example, but one well worth using. Thus, I am arguing here that at least because of this critical aspect of the kingdom of God—that Jesus went about doing good—Christians must be committed to the same, and must consider all the available proper means. Indeed, Matthew 4:23, perhaps, can be taken to be a concise but beautiful picture of the Christian mission in the world: "Jesus was going throughout all Galilee, teaching in their synagogues and proclaiming the gospel of the kingdom, and healing every kind of disease and every kind of sickness among the people." Galatians 2:10 also presents this wholistic picture of the Christian task. Again, then, a key aspect of the mission of Jesus is to do good in the world, to both body and soul, as we will explore more fully later. And if political means can be legally and peacefully utilized for this purpose, it may indeed be sin *not* to so utilize them! But there are, to be sure, inherent temptations in this way of thinking. And this leads us to a final point.

4. *Christians must constantly guard against exchanging or mistaking the kingdom of Christ for the kingdoms of earth.* The reason I include this point is simple: I believe Christians in western countries, or at least in America, are constantly making this mistake. I have already argued, and I think it undeniable, that Christians must be wholly committed, from the heart, to what Christ is committed to. These things are laid out for us clearly in Scripture. They are, in fact, beautifully laid out in the two greatest commandments: love to God and love to man. But how easy it is to get sidetracked here! For we live in seductive times. We live in an age of virtually unprecedented prosperity and peace. We have more freedom and leisure available to us, perhaps, then any society in history. The subtle danger is to get too comfortable in this life. And we have all done it. None of us has escaped this snare. We are all marked by sinful levels of love and devotion to the good things of this life; how foolish it would be to deny it! Comfort, ease, entertainment, recreation, sport, fine food and drink, sexual gratification: we are so far past anything that even remotely resembles the sacrificial life of Jesus that it is almost unbelievable. Indeed, we all constantly need to consider whether

we are even truly following Jesus! And thus when we discuss the matter of politics, we need to be absolutely clear: once again, for the true Christian, political involvement should be *for the sake of the kingdom of Christ alone*. It must not be to serve our own interests. Prioritizing the kingdom of earth over the kingdom of heaven, then, can perhaps be defined as just this: seeking our own well-being instead of the interests of Christ and the good of others.

It must be emphasized once again that these are two different kingdoms, with radically different pursuits and aims. And we dare not attempt to dogmatically posit a relationship between the two, and especially not an essential one. The kingdom of Christ and the success of his mission have *never* been tied to or dependent on any political power or even any particular earthly state of affairs. No form of government, however evil, and no lack of freedom, have ever hindered its success. To claim otherwise would be to blaspheme against the sovereign power of God! And as the Word of God plainly shows in the lives of the apostles, and as even the testimony of history makes plain, whenever political authorities have tried to stop God's people or stamp out his truth, it has only increased or spread all the more. We dare not thus think that the Christian mission *depends* on any political entity, such as any amount of freedom. How absurd. The sovereign power of God is not hindered by the affairs of men; indeed, it is his sovereign power that often ordains the loss of earthly freedom! Thus, utilization of any political means is subordinate to our real purpose, which is to advance the gospel or to do good to others; and when this means is frustrated, we do not give up. We rest in the sovereignty of God, and we return ever more fervently to prayer.

The question might arise, then, regarding what to do when a righteous, Christ-centered effort to do good to others is thwarted by the powers that be. And here we would do well to add a caveat to what we have said. The mission of Christ indeed includes doing good in the world. But the achievement of the earthly well-being of others is ultimately a *secondary good*. We must be careful here, for I do not mean to suggest that seeking the well-being of those in need is necessarily a secondary *priority*, as we will see in the next chapter. But it is clearly to be considered a secondary good by all followers of Jesus. The evidence for this incredibly important distinction is clear in the Word of God. Persecution and suffering will come to all of God's people, and we must patiently bear it (John 15:20, 2 Tim 3:12). Indeed, we are to consider ourselves blessed when we do so (Matt 5:11–12)! To make earthly justice, blessing, security, comfort, and health more important than salvation, discipleship, holiness, etc., is to miss Christ's gospel message entirely. Thus, those who are his followers in this life must pursue earthly blessing with a degree of sober, eternally-focused awareness: full and final freedom for the oppressed; real prosperity; ultimate security; perfect health; lasting happiness; all of these are reserved for heaven! We cannot so pursue these things, politically or otherwise, that we forget that God has not guaranteed them for the here and now. And we dare not be ultimately discouraged by the loss of earthly goods. The greatest and truest good concerns eternal salvation and future blessing, not blessing in the here and now.

POLITICS: THE PROBLEM REVISITED

The temptation for all Christians is to misconstrue these things. Indeed, the human heart inevitably drifts toward earthly concerns, and it is often hard to hold these issues in proper balance. But staying focused on Christ's kingdom means that we don't mistake the earthly for the heavenly. So here, I want to move toward a conclusion in this chapter by considering ways in which Christians are doing just that—justifying their political involvement by pursuing things that patently are not things that Jesus pursued. Indeed, political involvement among Evangelicals here in America has gotten to the point that many claim that the Bible directs us to promote and pursue a certain kind of economic system, maximum freedom, and a particular form of government, among other things. These notions, above most today, it seems, are those which appear most likely to lure their adherents into an exchange of earthly and heavenly kingdoms.

But can such claims even be taken seriously? I ask this because a straightforward and honest study of the life of Jesus and his apostles, as well as a reading of the entire New Testament, makes such claims appear rather bizarre. To insinuate for even a moment that our Lord, who gave up preoccupation with every earthly thing, including food and drink, to do the will of his Father, would ever be concerned with something so absurdly contrary to everything he ever did and taught as economics, earthly freedom, or government systems, is, again, borderline blasphemous. And this is not to mention the apostles, who were consumed with the same mission: the spread of Christ's love and truth to the ends of the earth, to the utter neglect or concern for earthly powers or worldly affairs.

The general New Testament duty of Christians toward government is simple: obey it, unless it commands you expressly to disobey God (Acts 4:19–20). Earthly government is ordained by God, and the specific rulers are put in place by God himself (Rom 13:1). The topic is mentioned in passing in only a few places, and the message in every passage is the same. Furthermore, it could certainly be argued that a primary motivation behind the passages could be stated as follows: don't make government obedience an issue, because disobeying the government will inevitably detract from the witness and cause of Christ in the world. This is certainly a possible takeaway from Jesus's words in Matthew 22:15–22, where he neatly dismisses the Pharisees on the matter of taxes; and it seems to be the clear lesson of the passages on government written by Paul and Peter in Romans 13:1–7 and 1 Peter 2:13–17, the latter passage expressly wishing that those who speak badly of Christians will be silenced. Indeed, I have no problem at all claiming on the New Testament evidence that matters of earthly politics *clearly* and *obviously* are not the business of the Christian. Of course, it has been argued incessantly that our modern world, with its new-found emphasis on democratic processes, with its new opportunities for political involvement for all, has changed things, as we have mentioned. But of course it hasn't. God's word is not incomplete, or its teaching relative to time and place. God's people are not to change their focus. Earthly priorities are still not our aim. We are to be about preaching the gospel and doing good to all, as disciples of Christ; and we are to have respect for and to obey the rulers and authorities on earth. As we have said, political involvement may be warranted biblically—but only if it is in the service of the mission of Jesus.

Often, of course, it is God's will to allow earthly governments to become corrupt and even antithetical to the mission of Christ. Does that mean, then, that Christians then have the right to become engrossed in politics, in order to effect government change? Certainly it does not. When legal, peaceful, and not too distracting, certainly some involvement in these things may be warranted; but once again, we must keep our proper aim in view, as we said above. But how easy it is to turn shifting grains of biblical evidence into unassailable mountains of proof! The human heart is so prone to self-deception. And this leads us to the arguments themselves. I have actually heard Christians passionately defend the duty of promoting capitalism on such slender evidence as the 8th commandment—since God says we shouldn't steal, then men and women at all times are entitled to property; thus, the argument inevitably runs, we must promote the protection of private property as a God-ordained good. Such thinking is painfully ignorant of the flow of biblical revelation. Jesus called us as his followers to give up our earthly property in order to follow him. He told us as clearly and definitely as possible to avoid all covetousness, as we have seen. He also bid us give up all our earthly freedom for his service. No Christian, then, should take the serious pursuit or promotion of such things as private property or earthly freedom to be warranted by Jesus. It may not be *wrong* to advocate for such at times or to vote for certain policies, especially if one thinks they will ultimately be best for all people, and if certain government regimes are becoming genuinely oppressive of those in need—but to go so far as to argue that the Bible mandates or calls us to pursue or promote such earthly blessings, especially compared to how fervently we should pursue and promote the truth and mission of Christ, is, again, misguided, and terribly so. Those who argue thus are either not reading the New Testament at all or are deceiving themselves. Of course, many Christians have allowed American political thinking to infiltrate their theology, as we all know. But once again, to insist that such things as property, earthly liberty, and the pursuit of earthly happiness are inalienable rights given by God, that we must demand for ourselves and others, is, to be frank, a direct contradiction to the teaching of Jesus. Jesus called us to something radical and undeniably new—the sacrifice of *everything* to his person and cause. This is what the inauguration of the kingdom of heaven brings.

There may in fact be wrong thinking or even misguided theology behind such claims; but the real culprit, I fear again, is our own worldly desires. The same can certainly be argued of those who passionately advocate for a certain view of government. In a story that is now well-known, since the 80s and the rise of the Religious Right, the Republican Party and Christianity have often been firmly linked in the American Evangelical world. But surely this is similarly misguided. Jesus is not to be associated with any political party, especially one built as much on economic interests as it is on public morality. How disgraceful. If the Democratic Party, despite its heinous moral failures, is known as the party that helps the poor and the stranger, then how in the world can the Republican Party be considered the party of Jesus? What we have, frankly, is a dangerous and deceptive lie being promoted by many in the professing Evangelical church. In the supposed name of Jesus, but actually in the name, I fear, of earthly liberty and economic prosperity—the twin pillars of the Right—the so-called Christian Right has hijacked the Bible and taken it hostage to its self-serving claims. The result is a large number of Christians who are no longer capable of seeing how they have been deceived. The world has indeed tamed the church, as Hauerwas and Willimon claim.

So I contend strongly that Christians have no biblical warrant at all for claiming that capitalism, economic freedom, limited government, or any other treasured notion of the Right should be pursued as part of our foundational calling, which is to follow Jesus as true disciples. The New Testament is abundantly clear, in the example and teaching of our Lord and the apostles, and in his call to discipleship, what our calling is in the kingdom of heaven, and how we should view these particular matters. Capitalism may be the preferred system in many contexts, though I think the matter far more complex than most Evangelicals make it; regardless, the matter is ultimately irrelevant for followers of Jesus. Earthly freedom may be a marvelous blessing, but it, too, is ultimately immaterial to the business of following Jesus, since we are now his bondservants. Limited government may be desirable in some sense, but what does this mean? That governments should never help the poor or have certain compassionate policies in place? There is simply no clear biblical support for such conclusions. In fact, when one reads the Old Testament, when God's purposes were directly involved with the things of earth through the nation of Israel, quite the opposite seems to be the case.[9] And arguments that are often made in support of limited government usually make the same mistake: they attempt to prescribe the full-orbed responsibilities of government from biblical passages with very narrow scope and application. To argue thus is blatantly to disregard the basic interpretive principles of context and intention.

Of course, we could go on and on, and seek to overturn every single argument raised in support of the political views that are commonly heard in the Evangelical church, but the vast majority of them simply are not worth taking seriously. Yes, we should engage with the political system for

---

9. I find J.P. Moreland's contention that the example of Old Testament Israel is irrelevant to the discussion to be rather desperate; see Moreland, "A Biblical Case," https://tifwe.org/wp-content/uploads/2013/04/JP-Moreland-Limited-Govt.pdf. Neither do I find his use of the biblical evidence in the least compelling, as he seems to make the mistake mentioned here—that of stretching verses clearly beyond their context and intention.

doing good as Jesus defines it; but which political party has a clear handle on the ethics of Jesus is, in the end, somewhat questionable. The Left has gone completely morally haywire, to be sure, endorsing all sorts of wickedness; but they seem to have the most compassion for the poor, the stranger, and the oppressed, groups we are constantly directed to care for in the Word of God, just as Jesus did. The Right is more set against abortion, and less enamored with the claims of the so-called LGBTQ+ movement—though that may be changing—but they also seem intent on riches and economic prosperity, often to the neglect of the needy, which is also despicable in the sight of God. Carl Trueman surely speaks wisdom here:

> The problem is, of course, that whether there is a distinctly biblical position on these matters that can thus be pressed on the church is debatable . . . Sure, there are basic elements to Christian ethics: respect for life, honesty, care for the poor, etc.; and in preaching the gospel week by week, the church shapes the minds and ethics of her people; but how these things manifest themselves at the level of political policy is something with which Christians, as members of civic society, have to wrestle with and over which they can legitimately disagree. The danger in taking strong political positions on these issues, and even worse, partisan political positions, is that the church will ultimately exclude those who do indeed believe the gospel and who should therefore be included.[10]

Thus, says Trueman, even if one wanted to have discussions over political policy, it would be dubious indeed whether one could utilize the Word of God to support any one party exclusively.

Again, Jesus came to do physical good to those in need, without question; and it is indeed a difficult issue, at times, to know how much political effort one should undertake on behalf of such genuinely oppressed groups. This is a question we will return to in the next chapter. But for now, I say again: to claim the right to get involved in politics on behalf of the very things Jesus called us to surrender for the sake of his person and mission is blatantly misguided. In this sense, again, the issue of politics is both simple and clear. It truly makes one wonder whether people have really met Jesus at all, or are truly following him. All that remains, then, is that these are idols—idols of self-interest. They are things we care about more than Christ and others.

---

10. Truman, *Republocrat*, 107.

Jesus didn't come to grant us earthly rights or freedoms—he called us to surrender our earthly rights and freedoms and live for heaven. I say it again: if political involvement is to be undertaken at all—and I allow that often it indeed should be in our modern world—it should be for one purpose only for the true disciple: to help carry out the mission of Jesus. Daniel Williams states this point well:

> The Bible is quite clear that God has already established a political order, and it is called the "kingdom of God". . . But it is a kingdom that God brought about not through conquest or majority vote but through the weakness of the cross, and it is a kingdom that Jesus's followers enter by dying to themselves and suffering for the sake of the kingdom (2 Thess 1:5). Just as Jesus was glorified through the shame of the cross, so, too, will his followers glorify God and reveal God's kingdom to others when they die to themselves (John 12:23–26). The cross gives a radically different rationale for Christian political participation, because it demonstrates that we do not win through displays of power . . . Our task is simply to reveal God's kingdom to others, something that we do in our daily work, in our conversations with others, and even in the voting booth. We can do this by showing in some small measure what God's righteous order might look like—a demonstration that is probably best accomplished by a demonstration of love for our neighbor. If the sovereign king of God's kingdom declared that the second greatest commandment—a commandment that summarized all of God's law governing interpersonal relations in the political sphere—was to love our neighbor as ourselves (Matt 22:39–40), then we can safely assume that one of the central ways that we can reveal God's kingdom to others through politics is to vote in such a way that shows the maximum amount of love for our neighbors even if (and maybe especially if) this means voting against our own self-interest.[11]

It is hard not to affirm these words with a hearty "Amen!" When it comes to political involvement—if and when we are to engage in it—Christ and others, always, should be our priority, and not ourselves. Above all, may God give us a spirit of wisdom and self-discernment, so that we would stop rationalizing our obsession with political and earthly affairs and begin truly and deeply to involve ourselves with the true mission of Christ, and with love to our fellow man!

---

11. Williams, *Politics*, Introduction.

6

Causes

It was a cool, cloudless morning in a large Asian city known for its spectacular weather; neither the dust nor the grim, tattered buildings could keep out the dazzling early sun. It was a day of promise. I stepped onto the campus of the large urban university where I was teaching a class on western film to an eager, but inevitably disappointed, class of one hundred or so students from all over the country (they wanted *Star Wars*; I gave them *Sunset Boulevard*). But as I walked into the courtyard of my towering new classroom building, my blood froze.

There, in a crumpled heap midst a pile of garbage—the scattered limbs indistinguishable from the scraps of litter—lay the broken body of a student who had obviously leaped to his death some time during the night. Suicide was common in this country, I knew; but to see it up close and personal on a day like this—ripe with promise, like the students themselves, and from among the very ones I was desperately trying to reach with a message of hope—rattled me to my core.

I found out later that the suspected cause was an incredibly sad one. Just a few days earlier, an Asian movie star, one known to have had struggles with depression and also gender identity, had leaped to his death from a luxurious hotel balcony in Hong Kong. Rumor ran rampant that this student was experiencing that same conflict. I had already encountered depression here, but little did I know at the time, struggles with gender identity and sexuality were already a major issue in this country.

And over the next few years, I was to encounter quite a bit of it, and would have to work hard to minister effectively in what was undoubtedly a rapidly and rather tragically modernizing third-world context.

One young student in my class called himself "Boggle." Despite his dubious choice of name, Boggle was an incredibly gifted young man, intelligent, well-spoken, clean cut, and clearly confident. On the first day of our English class, I asked if anyone wished to introduce themselves. Boggle jumped up and headed to the front of the classroom, where he proceeded not only to introduce himself, but to launch into what was for all intents and purposes a crusade speech in favor of same-sex relationships. At that time in the early millennium, and especially in that closed and still outwardly conservative country, it was a moment of almost breathtaking bravery. And foolhardiness. For neither Boggle's classmates that day nor his larger peer group, I was to find out later, were very accepting of his views. Eventually realizing that Boggle himself likely struggled with these issues, I resolved to pray for him in particular over the course of the year. But the year didn't last long for Boggle. He was eventually kicked out of the school for bizarre behavior, including repeatedly bringing girls into his dorm room, obviously against the rules. In subsequent discussions with other students, however, the picture that emerged was that Boggle was engaging in such behavior to stifle far more serious rumors about him—rumors that he was gay. Hearing this deeply troubling information, my heart sank. I resolved to track him down and have at least one opportunity to speak to him, which I eventually did. I'll never forget that occasion—looking into the face of this incredibly gifted, deeply sensitive young man, who was obviously struggling with issues that were far beyond him—and of all things in a country that was hostile both to him and to Christianity. He kept appealing to America, my own country, to defend himself, holding it up as a beacon of tolerance and virtue. Each time I had to gently counter that America on the whole had, sadly, pursued freedom and acceptance far beyond what God intended. I eventually preached the gospel to him as clearly as I did to anyone in that country. And then I left, never to see him again, hopeful that this one encounter might be enough for God to use. Only God knows where he is now.

There were many others. I think of Mary, a young student whose desire for a same-sex relationship was preventing her from following Jesus. Thank God, at least, that she got it right that such behavior was unacceptable for Christians. But no one exemplified these struggles like the young man I'll call Peter. Peter had befriended my sister, who was also teaching in Asia, and Peter and I became friends as well. Peter was something different in that country. Most of these city kids were already spoiled anyway, third-world country notwithstanding, but Peter's dad was genuinely wealthy, even by American standards. Peter was raised in a life of genuine privilege, and he would eventually take up residence in the United States, albeit under dubious circumstances. After a year or so of becoming friends in his home country, one day Peter invited me to a new movie, an exciting American martial arts movie that was being simultaneously released in both countries. It was a big deal around the world, so I was curious enough to attend. When we entered the theatre, however, I noticed something odd. There were no seats, only couches—two-person ones. And there was only one couch left, right in the middle. As I followed Peter rather embarrassingly to the couch, I took a look around; every other couch was occupied by a heterosexual couple. I was beginning to have an odd feeling.

During the opening credits, I ran it by Peter. Yes, it was a "couples" theatre. Yes, we were the only two of the same sex sitting together. But wouldn't these people think we were a romantic couple, I asked? Yes, and so what? was Peter's reply. It was then that it began to dawn on me what a fool I'd been. Peter, he would go on to tell me later, was gay, and he had been pursuing me for more than friendship the whole time. Despite this somewhat complicating factor, over the years that followed, I maintained a close friendship with Peter and shared the gospel with him many times. I counseled with the friends who became painfully aware of his chosen lifestyle. I even continued to advise Peter after he immigrated to the United States. Eventually, however, he rejected the gospel, definitively and multiple times.

What was going on in these students' lives in a far-away developing country, of course, has been going on in arguably a much more magnified way in western countries. What we are dealing with is nothing less than a massive social crisis that has long been underway and shows no signs of abating. And as we now know in the Christian world, professing Christians all around us are caving on the issue, while others simply don't know how to handle it or what to think of it. We need wisdom and balance here, as always, but such has been notoriously difficult to maintain on this and other social issues. Thus, I wish to spend this chapter briefly discussing and exploring this and two other critical social issues that the church is facing, and hopefully provide a few biblical insights and some direction about the way to proceed.

THE LGBTQ+ MOVEMENT

The enormous swell of pro-LGBTQ+ sentiment washing over our culture is threatening to drown the church. That the swell has already claimed many prominent professed Christians, as well as local churches and even entire denominations, might be cast, I contend, as a good thing; if the LGBTQ+ movement is becoming, as indeed I think it is, a sort of identity marker of fidelity to genuine Christianity, then so be it. Let it indeed divide the false church from the true; it is always good to weed the garden.

There is no need, of course, to deny the reality of a genetic component to same-sex attraction. We are born in sin, and this surely includes everything from conception on. I personally would welcome a bit more sanctified speculation on what this means theologically: certainly, God made Adam and Eve by hand; but he obviously foresaw that future combinations of genes would result in male and female offspring that would be on some occasions less "purely" masculine or feminine, right? And thus with tendencies toward aberrant desires? Is this, then, what being born in sin means: that God is no longer directly involved in the process? I do indeed believe that such withdrawal on God's part is a significant result of the Fall. In philosophy, when we discuss the problem of evil, the devastating effects of man being forced out of the garden, away from and out from under God's sovereign and loving protection, are things we must take most seriously. But no doubt there is much more to this conversation; perhaps Adam and Eve were originally composed of body, soul, and Holy Spirit, with the latter no longer being part of the process after the Fall. For now, only God knows the full truth.

But it is similarly unquestionable, in my view, that culture has played a part in this whole issue. "Nurture" has long been known to play a significant part in anyone's development, and it is widely known that even secular associations such as the APA take the following stance:

> There is no consensus among scientists about the exact reasons that an individual develops a heterosexual, bisexual, gay or lesbian orientation. Although much research has examined the possible genetic, hormonal, developmental, social and cultural influences on sexual orientation, no findings have emerged that permit scientists to conclude that sexual orientation is determined by any particular factor or factors. Many think that

nature and nurture both play complex roles; most people experience little or no sense of choice about their sexual orientation.[1]

This last statement I have verified from numerous personal experiences with people who feel this way; again, we need not wonder about it. I am not saying, of course, that such people are always right about the things they assert based on feelings; there is no question that in addition to an insistence on the biological origin of homosexual attraction, the larger pro-gay movement has worked hard to establish the various letters of the current acronym as strict categories, an assertion that is surely dogmatic. But there is no need to revisit the debate over gender fluidity here. I think it significant indeed that nurture and culture are still considered by even many secular scientists to play important roles. This fits well with biblical sociological descriptions such as those we find in Romans 1, and I think it naive to think it hasn't happened in our own society.

What might be the cultural culprits, then? It is certainly beyond the scope of this book and my own expertise to attempt to say too much on the matter, but I can't help but at least draw some attention to the gradual blurring of gender lines in the culture at large, including everything from traditional roles, serious challenges regarding which go back at least several hundred years in the West, to dress or standards of clothing, which have gradually become less and less distinct, to general behavior expectations. If nurture indeed plays a part on developing brains, as surely it does, then obviously the loss of standards regarding behavior, dress, and roles can do nothing but speed along or intensify the problems for those with certain tendencies and inclinations. But I think we can go further; surely, as many theologians have pointed out, the incessant trend of western society in general toward more and more degrees of emotionalism, subjectivism, sensuality, etc., which are now part of the very fabric of every single atmosphere we inhabit in our daily lives from the cradle on, plays an important part. Human beings today experience far more emotionally and sensually, surely, than those in the past. This surely stems from many factors, including modern conveniences, increasing living standards and technological advances leading to greater leisure and more and more intense physical experiences, a general decline in public standards and barriers, etc. That these changes have occurred I believe is undeniable. And they are surely explicable on some level.

---

1. "Sexual Orientation and Homosexuality," *American Psychological Association*, https://www.apa.org/topics/lgbtq/orientation.

A possible partial explanation is as follows: social change reflects what individuals naturally tend to in the absence of mitigating and opposing factors, and physical pleasure, in particular sexual gratification, is perhaps the most powerful driving force of all, at least in societies with a reasonably comfortable standard of living. Again, Romans 1 bears this out powerfully, but here we are more concerned with changes within the human psyche. I don't wish to attempt to fly beyond my airspace here, but it surely seems as if those in the West several generations ago were not nearly as in touch with their own subjectivity as people are today. They were, perhaps, far less given to or driven by pleasure or their emotions; and they certainly were far more swayed by what we might call traditional ideals. What we have, then, is, as Freud would put it, a shrinking or shifting set of standards in our collective superego. What has emerged is a set of bizarre results: souls today are overstimulated, over-gratified, overly self-occupied, and certainly overly introspective, at least where their emotions are concerned; while at the same time they are needier and less fulfilled than ever.

I believe the significance of this for the LGBTQ+ movement is profound. Obviously, the more subjective space, so to speak, an individual is free to explore, the further one will instinctively go; such is our natural tendency. And if certain tendencies are present, then these tendencies will ultimately be satisfied with nothing less than full realization if they are allowed or even encouraged by society to seek such. This same basic principle is easily demonstrated in sexual perversion, in which one is no longer capable of being stimulated by things one has already experienced, and seeks out new and different experiences; but I think it has even more profound implications for the whole matter of subjectivity and gender identity. Human beings are just that malleable; and in our present society, where many traditional moral barriers can no longer be found, it is no wonder that souls have gotten to such extremes in our world. If we could state the problem succinctly from a Christian point of view: human beings need God-appointed social and psychological boundaries. And they need to be taught to think that these boundaries are there because they should be. Such needs to be a significant part of their nurture. But the exact opposite is the case today, and this decline has been in operation, of course, for hundreds of years. In fact, it may be that the subjective space or climate, so to speak, around young people in our society today, with which they are bombarded on a daily basis, is too great for any private, family-based nurture to overcome. It truly is a problem.

Of course, these are largely theoretical thoughts, and not ultimately germane to our subject. For the question, as always, is what the Bible says. And here I would simply say that I think it is undeniably and unquestionably clear that the Bible forbids homosexual desires and behavior. As has been ably pointed out by many, it is condemned explicitly not only in multiple Old and New Testament passages, but implicitly by the Bible's presentation of the sacred distinction between male and female, marriage, procreation, etc. There is simply no way to affirm homosexuality in any way, shape, or form biblically. I have seen no counter argument that is even worth taking seriously. Add to this the fact that, as is also pointed out frequently, to even question the Bible's stance on this is to go against two thousand years of unified Christian understanding on the matter. So, theologically speaking, the project of reinterpreting the Bible on this point is doomed to fail. There is really nothing else to say here.

What remains, then, is to try and deal with the enormously tragic and difficult practical matter of same-sex attraction in both the unevangelized and the struggling believer. And here I would like simply to point out again that balance, as always, is desperately needed, but balance is tragically not often found. Some professed Christian churches have failed completely by affirming homosexual behavior as acceptable, thus demonstrating, sadly, that they have none of the Holy Spirit's guidance on this issue. Others, however, have become so welcoming to those struggling that at times it appears that they that are capitulating. Still others have no sensitivity for this struggle at all.

But surely balance *can* be found. The solution, as always, is to seek the heart of Christ through the power of the Holy Spirit. Our Lord exemplified both perfect compassion and perfect zeal for God's standards of holiness. We must—I repeat, must—hold such aberrations as same-sex attraction with an appropriate level of Spirit-filled dismay, deep sadness, and even shame. However, we must also reach people with an ever-embracing, ever-caring, and deeply-tender love. Some sins *are* expressions of greater levels of distance from the will of God. And yet Jesus dealt with all sinners the same. Some Christians need to get out of their small-town mindsets and remind themselves that such issues go all the way back to the beginning of human society. Others need to remember that such sins are serious and even extreme expressions of the judgment of God on a culture (Rom 1: 18–32). As always, we need great measures of the Holy Spirit to find the balance.

I would like to offer two additional comments here. One, I have a concern over the debate that is ongoing in Evangelical circles about same-sex attraction. Surely they are right who say that same-sex *tendencies* do not necessarily equal sin in and of themselves; they may be the result of the Fall, but they are not sin unless someone *experiences* same-sex attraction, let alone gives into it. What is also surely right, however, is that same-sex attraction itself, if actually felt or experienced, *is* sin, regardless of whether one gives into it or not. The same is certainly true of *any* feeling one has that is contrary to God's will and design, such as feelings of attraction one may experience toward someone they are not married to, however slight. But I wonder if theologians are treating same-sex attraction with unnecessary strictness here—a strictness they are not willing to apply to these other illicit feelings? Heterosexual men, if they are not full of the Holy Spirit, often have to fight the feeling or experience of attraction toward images of women or women in real life they encounter. My point is this: are theologians treating such feelings with the same degree of strictness and absoluteness they are asking of those who are same-sex attracted? It may seem, to some, that heterosexuals should have more leeway because their desires are less aberrant; but for those who are genuinely same-sex attracted, and feel to some degree that they were born that way, the feeling is obviously just as instinctual. I suppose what I am getting at is that there seems to be a double-standard in operation at times. But there must not be. Heterosexual Christians (and theologians!) have to maintain the same level of watchfulness, and the same zero-tolerance policy, so-to-speak, toward their own illicit attractions that homosexual people do. I hope this awareness can be maintained; if not, we are certainly guilty of prejudice and a double-standard. It's simple, really: Jesus requires the same level of holiness for all of us.

A final thought: it all comes back to discipleship. Having counseled with young men and women who struggle with these issues, it never fails to hit me that for those who are truly oriented toward same-sex attraction and yet wish to follow Christ, the road will be hard. Giving up the possibility of experiencing one of the greatest blessings on earth, romantic intimacy, is a cross few of us would be willing to bear, no doubt. Such souls and their struggles need to be handled with the utmost sympathy and sensitivity. There is also a warning. Many have departed from the faith over this struggle, or have compromised their beliefs, unwilling to accept that God could ask them to do something so excruciatingly difficult. Let us then turn the spotlight back on ourselves: do we understand how serious our Lord is about all of us following him? We pity those with these struggles, perhaps, but ultimately care not for their pain, while privately indulging in things we know Jesus has warned us against. When we ask those struggling with same-sex attraction to deny themselves something so personal, so central to human life and experience—while we acknowledge, of course, that one's identity should not be fully bound up with one's sexual desires or perceived gender—are we also acknowledging how Jesus calls *us*, as well, to deny our most basic desires? Our natural, sinless ambition, perhaps (if there is such a thing), or our desire for power over others (our sinful ambition), or our covetousness, or our fear and anxiety, or our own illicit desires? God help us all to realize that Jesus is calling us *all* to give him *everything*. Only with such a realization, and a striving after this ideal in our own lives, can we legitimately ask others to do the same. For all who are truly following Christ, the road is incredibly hard. Perhaps if many in the Evangelical church were truly denying themselves, taking up their crosses, and following Jesus in everyday life, they would have more sympathy for those whose struggles they so often disdain.

SOCIAL JUSTICE

I grew up—from ages five to twenty-two—in a small city in Northwest Louisiana. My parents, firm believers that Christians should not withdraw from the world, refused to put us in Christian schools or to homeschool us. We attended public schools from the beginning, and despite being exposed to a large amount of sin from an early age, it was a wonderful experience (or perhaps that was the reason). More than anything else in those days, especially because the neighborhood where the schools were located was rather poor, all the schools we attended were incredibly diverse. We also grew up playing sports, one of the great family legacies. In these realms, I was rubbing shoulders with children of other races from the very beginning. I absolutely loved it. My best friend in elementary school was a mixed-race child with a Thai heritage. My best friend in middle-school was an African-American boy (who turned out to have gender struggles). And though I attended one year of high school in a private Christian school to play sports with my brother, I quickly returned to public schools the following year. The all-white private Christian school we had attended was founded in the civil-rights era when integration became the law. Racism still lingered there, horribly so. I hated it.

My family had always been different. My grandfather had first run for governor on a segregationist platform, but soon reverted to his roots, his true soul, when the civil rights era came full circle. He is now known as a pro-civil rights governor. This made sense; he grew up poor, hitching rides to work after World War II in the back of pick-up trucks full of black laborers on their way to the cotton fields. There was, and still is, a camaraderie between all those mired in poverty; it has been my experience, at least in many rural Louisiana areas, that the lower you go on the poverty scale, the less racism you find. Most people aren't low enough to find this out. Sports helped too. My father practically lived in locker rooms all the way up to the NFL, and black athletes remained some of his best friends for years. In our church, we pursued diversity even when we were starting out. Caring for the oppressed was my parents' burden from the beginning, and this indeed became our legacy later, when my mother began operating an NPO aimed at helping women and children from oppressed minority groups in Asia. Working on behalf of such groups, you could say, is something we have given our whole lives to.

The point of all of this is simple, really: few things are more reprehensible to my family and me than a failure to take seriously the plight of oppressed peoples, especially minority groups. Those of us raised in the Deep South know that racism still exists, and that the power structures put in play in the twentieth century to keep black people out of public society have had powerful repercussions to this very day. Some just don't want to admit it. The city I grew up in was right next to a larger city that is home to one of the largest and neediest black communities anywhere in the United States. The church we joined before leaving for Asia, after my father's church eventually disbanded, sits at the doorstep of that community, and is still trying to reach it for Christ. It is a needy, oppressed community. Frankly speaking, those who pontificate about racism without any first-hand experience of it need to keep silent. Again, there is simply no getting around the facts: minority groups in our country, especially black people, have been horribly mistreated and oppressed in our country in times past; and that oppression continues to have effects in our day. This contention, especially the latter aspect, is so obvious in communities in the South that there is really no need to defend it.

Yet I do not wish to dive deeply into the debate about the extent of structural racism today; matters such as critical race theory and the like have received, in my view, far too much attention in the church already. No, denominations should not utilize such theories wholesale; clearly they inevitably make claims, draw conclusions, or promote ideologies that conflict with the Word of God. But I see no reason why such theories cannot be utilized in part, or with a hearty degree of judiciousness. If critical race theory has something true to say, let it be heard. Its critics are often the ones who proclaim the loudest that "all truth is God's truth," while similarly rejecting the percipient observations of Marx, the insights and advances of Freud and psychology in general, and many of the undeniable conclusions of science and philosophy. Evangelicalism continues to be mired in ignorance; this is virtually undeniable. What is fueling their fears on the matter of social justice, perhaps, is the same thing that always fuels the fears of those who are not truly living for the kingdom of heaven: the loss of their present way of life, with its comforts and privileges. And if this is the very thing that a theory calls into question, then why would Christians be bothered with it? It is incredible to me how the fears of the middle class, even (or especially) the Christian middle class, always, somehow, lead back to talk of socialism or Marxism. It is a bit ironic that those who trumpet the loudest against Marx may be those in the greatest danger of lending credence to his first major claim in the *Communist Manifesto*, that the history of society is really the history of class struggle. Indeed, such base desires *have* been a primary motivating force in history; is it really a surprise that the middle and upper classes are so afraid of such things as critical race theory? What we need, as always, is a Spirit-empowered return to discipleship; a newfound, fresh release of all that we possess and value to the lordship of Jesus Christ. Then we can proceed without all the unsanctified panic over theories.

The term "social justice" is similarly under attack, even from pastors and theologians who seem otherwise balanced. And as I will seek to point out in a moment, there is a balance to be had, for sure. But many of those who are leading the charge against this movement are not, in my view, giving satisfactory recognition to what is an essential part of the kingdom of God. And thus here, at last, we need briefly to consider this crucial aspect of the "physical" side of Jesus's mission, which we have begun exploring in the last couple of chapters, but which here I wish to finally bring into full view.

There is a standard claim in Evangelicalism that one often hears today, and it is this: there are *priorities* when it comes to advancing Christ's kingdom. Though Christ went about both preaching the gospel and doing good, when all is said and done, the former should be prioritized over the latter. Some advocates point to the life of Jesus to support such claims, or imply that the notion is simply logical; others appear to conflate the doing of good with attempts to establish a Christian political or social order, something we have already seen is misguided.[2] But while the notion that there should be priorities in the mission of Christ may seem correct on some isolated biblical evidence, such as the Great Commission—which doesn't explicitly mention the physical aspects of Jesus work—my contention here is that it is a bit misguided to speak of priorities. Clarifications are in order, and these things need to be carefully parsed out. Indeed, I fear that holding to such a model has led some in our day to neglect doing good altogether—which has no doubt compromised their witness for Christ.

The simple truth is this: Jesus didn't do physical good to establish a political order; he did it because it was right, and because he was filled with God's eternal compassion and love in the power of the Holy Spirit, which compelled him to meet people's physical needs. The following claim, then, I contend, is absolutely true based on the New Testament evidence, and should be maintained over and against a "priorities" model: doing good to those in need is an *essential*, or inseparable, element of the mission of Christ. To the degree that we are not doing such, then, to that degree we are not fulfilling the mission of Jesus. Of course, there may be certain ministries (or ministers) who have priorities,[3] but when one considers the church as a whole, meeting physical needs will always be an essential calling. This distinction—between certain ministries and the church on the whole—is an important one.

The biblical evidence for this claim is manifold. Preaching the gospel is, of course, likewise an essential element of the mission of Christ—notice, however, that the Great Commission requires us not to "preach the gospel," but to teach souls to observe "all that I commanded you"—but, tellingly, the gospel is to be preached, first and foremost, to those in need: "The Spirit of the Lord is upon me, because he anointed me to preach the gospel to the poor, he has sent me to proclaim release to the captives, and recovery of sight to the blind, to set free those who are oppressed, to proclaim the favorable year of the Lord" (Luke 4:18–19). In fulfilling this beautiful Old Testament promise, Jesus's mission here clearly is to target the needy and

---

2. See, for example, MacArthur, *Government*, 9–15.

3. One thinks, for example, of the apostles in Acts 6, which occasion led to the establishment of deacons.

oppressed with favor. Not only are they the first to get the gospel preached to them—surely a guiding principle for missions—but they are also to receive relief, release, recovery of sight, freedom, etc. And these are not merely symbolic claims; this was a literal part of what Jesus did. Verses 40 through 43 of the same chapter provide a beautiful picture of this integration: in verse forty, Jesus is patiently healing all those sick with various diseases, in verse 41, he is casting out demons, and in verse forty-three, he departs, saying that he must "preach the kingdom of God to the other cities also." Clearly, then, his preaching mission involves all these elements; all of this is to be pursued on behalf of "the kingdom of God."

It would be tedious indeed to list all the evidence in the gospels that this was an essential part of Jesus's mission. His care and favor for the poor, needy, and oppressed is recorded on nearly every page of the gospel accounts. And such concern is also clear in the labors of the apostles, who engaged in similar ministries of healing and concern for those in need.[4] Indeed, pressing deeper, Christ has even called us to *be* oppressed for his name. Part of this involves voluntarily suffering with others when they are in need. The New Testament calls us to such empathy on virtually every page. Thus, again, it is a bit misleading to speak of priorities. It is clear that Christ's mission involves, essentially, identification with and concern for these types of groups. Thus, I think it appropriate to say that whatever we can legally do for the poor, oppressed, sick, etc., in our communities, we Christians must be doing. To the degree that we are not doing this, then, to that degree we are not only failing to carry out the witness of Christ, but we may also be actually undermining the gospel before a watching world.

What a tremendous rebuke this is to many professed people of God, and to many churches and whole denominations! Jesus came not merely to preach abstract truths; he embodied the very love of God in the world, and he came expressly to demonstrate that love. This is what being salt and light means, indeed: doing the works of Jesus. What a shame that many Evangelicals today have failed to recapture this commitment to those in need. Compassion, service, charity, hospitality, companionship, support—all the things the Christian community should be doing—how little we see of such activity, especially in the Reformed community! Little wonder our evangelistic endeavors have been so ineffectual.

4. See, for example, Galatians 2:10, in which the apostles James, Cephas, and John give Paul and Barnabas their blessing, asking them only to "remember the poor—the very thing I also was eager to do."

Now, what then does this have to do with the social justice movement? The application should be obvious. Whether we wish to call it social justice or not—Christians are surely wasting time to be quibbling over the use of terms—the church must be committed to those who are oppressed. If minority groups are still being persecuted, mistreated, or denied opportunities; or if there is still prejudice or racism, systemic or otherwise; true Christians should be aware of these things, investigating these things, and working hard to overturn such things. Now, again, I am not here to make any statements with any degree of certainty regarding the pervasiveness of such things in our culture. As it stands, I am often appalled at the utter apathy many Christians have toward those in need, including minority groups. And I would be so bold to say that we don't necessarily need to get to the bottom of systemic racism to know that Christians are failing. Surely there has been systemic racism for some time in our culture; no one who has studied history would claim otherwise. Of course black Americans were left out and left behind, deliberately and definitively, by federal, state, and local governments after (ironically) their supposed emancipation in the 19th century. The evidence for this can easily be found. But our (mostly white) middle and upper middle classes are already, perhaps, in violation of Jesus's call to discipleship by their pursuit of wealth, security, comfort, etc. And they are often doing it to the neglect of those in need in their own societies. What is the point, then, of defending ourselves on systemic racism, or even of pursuing this question? We are already guilty of systemic neglect of the demands of Jesus, and if this is part of our contribution to systemic racism, then we need to acknowledge it. I pray to hear no more critique of critical theory, social justice, etc., until I actually hear it from someone who is putting their life and lifestyle on the line for Christ and those in need as a true disciple. Who is truly giving up all they are and possess to see those in need obtain relief from suffering and oppression, just as Jesus did? To this person I will listen.

There is, however, another side to this story. And it must be heard. Let us recall that Jesus did not challenge the political order in order to achieve his goals; his work toward deliverance had limits. We need to be aware of this fact, even while we use legitimate political means to achieve good in the world. But there is more. Jesus's essential mission included doing good to those in need, it is true. But for those who follow Jesus, there is a flip side, and I believe it holds a powerful truth that may in fact be a key to resolving this issue in the Christian community. That flip side is simply this: for followers of Jesus who are themselves oppressed, freedom from oppression is not, in fact, to be a priority! And *this,* I contend, is not being heard in the Christian community very much, especially from the black Christian community. One of the great truths of Christ, as we have already seen, is that in following him, we must take up our crosses. We must voluntarily take upon ourselves deprivation, loss, hardship, persecution, suffering, etc., for the sake of Christ, for such will come. We must voluntarily give up homes, families, financial security, etc. We must be willing to face all sorts of difficulty for the sake of Christ; and when we do so, we are blessed (Matt 5:10, 1 Pet 3:14). We are, in fact, to consider such suffering as joy (Jas 1:2). We should, indeed, be constantly looking not to earthly happiness and fulfillment, but to our better and lasting possession (Heb 10:34). Thus, here is an interesting paradox of sorts (though it is not formally a paradox, of course): Christians are to passionately pursue the well-being of others in need, in obedience to Christ, while simultaneously *not* pursuing their own well-being if they are oppressed! This is not to say that they should never pursue their own well-being, of course; we should seek to ease our suffering, and especially the suffering of those under our care, when we can, with whatever means we can. But this should not be our *priority*. The call of Christ to discipleship demands that we surrender earthly comforts for the greater call of serving Christ. In fact, this may be a sort of paradigmatic expression of what a Christian should be: a Christian is one who *gives things up* so that *others might gain*. The greatest of all is, indeed, a servant (Matt 23:11). This is why Christians are generally told in the New Testament not to seek their own welfare first, but that of others (1 Cor 10:33). This is, indeed, an essential part of what honoring Christ means: we are to seek *his* interests, not our own (Phil 2:21). And Christ's interests, clearly, are the will of his Father and those in need. This is why, in the famous parable of the sheep and the goats, Jesus tells us that when we help those in the body who are in need, we are serving, in essence, Christ himself (Matt 25:35–40).

The application here is obvious, but perhaps painful to hear. Yet it must be said. Christians, no matter whether they are truly oppressed, needy, or otherwise disadvantaged, are not to prioritize their own earthly relief, release, freedom, advantage, etc. They are, instead, to endure suffering with patience (1 Pet 2:18–24), and so find favor with God. In so doing, we are following in the footsteps of Jesus, this passage goes on to explain. Incredibly, in this very passage, the Apostle Peter applies these things to servants who have "unreasonable" or "perverse" masters (verse

18). And though slavery as practiced in biblical times was no doubt different than slavery in the modern era, and while slavery in the modern era was a disgusting, greed-driven, despicable activity in direct opposition to the revealed will of God throughout the Scriptures, the principle holds, whether we wish to acknowledge it or not: for Christians, earthly freedom is not more important to God than righteous suffering. Is seeking to obtain one's freedom, release, etc., wrong? Again, of course not; Paul clearly says one should obtain it if possible (1 Cor 7:21). Indeed, in this passage Paul makes it clear that earthly freedom is the preferred state due to the ultimate freedom that Christ has provided for us. But over and over again in the epistles, the message is clear: one's attitude under oppression is more important than deliverance from it. God might bring deliverance for his people, but often he doesn't. God's people have been known since Old Testament times for undergoing persecution and difficulty, and even horrible torture and death, for the sake of God (Heb 11:36–40), and in a righteous manner. In so doing, they are unique witnesses of God in the world. And our lot is to follow in their footsteps—even voluntarily, as we have said.

My point in all this is to ask this question: Have certain minority churches misplaced their priorities? This is hard to say, but I have to admit that at times it feels like it. Black professing Christians are supporting social justice causes in greater and greater numbers, even separating from white-dominated churches at times. The situation is surely complex; but I fear the temptation to care about earthly things has become too great for some black American Christians. So my message to the oppressed church is simply this: your identity is with Christ, and your full and final release, relief, freedom, etc., are in heaven! Your priority is not so much to crusade for earthly benefits and blessings, but to use your suffering, to whatever degree it is suffering, to demonstrate the patient, righteous faith that the Bible calls us to, while also using your situation as an opportunity to help others in need. Thus, I say again: the oppressing church may certainly be failing greatly in this matter, but the oppressed church may also be failing. Perhaps if both recalibrate themselves on their calling as disciples of Christ, we can finally begin to get some healing on this issue. Again, in my view black Christians have every right to be hurt, dismayed, confused, etc., and also to seek righteous ways to rectify injustice, both within the church and outside of it. But is this enough to cause them to turn against their fellow Christians, or to divide from them? Surely this is not being faithful to exemplify Christ in the midst of persecution. The burden of responsibility here may certainly be on the oppressing church, but I believe refocusing on the mission and call of Christ will help both groups find the middle ground. May God help us indeed to find it, and until we do, to seek his face on this issue as never before!

THE ROLE OF WOMEN: A GROWING CRISIS

I grew up in a family of strong and gifted women. My father's mother and her three sisters were legends in their small Louisiana hometown; smart, beautiful, talented, and strong-willed as all get-out, as we used to say down South. They were all such colorful personalities, too. My father's sister was herself a character, possessed of a large and vivacious personality, full of good humor and strong opinions. She was so much fun to be around. It is true, the South has colorful characters like no other place in America, perhaps. But it was my mother who inevitably stole the show in our family. All of her father's almost unbearably strong character traits, plus some of my grandmother's more tender ones, as I have said, somehow found themselves in her. It was an explosive combination indeed. But it was also a combination that seemed destined for spiritual accomplishment. We always wondered how God would use her. Now we know.

There have been many times, however, while observing my mother's rather dynamic ministry, that I have wondered about the role of women in ministry and in the church. Indeed, it was a question that came up often around the dinner table. And it is not one with an easy answer. Today, other than social justice, there could be no more explosive issue threatening to tear Evangelicalism apart. And it must be handled with sensitivity. Women with large and ostensibly successful ministries are leaving such denominations as the SBC and taking many with them. Women in some places are growing less and less content, and even Evangelical churches appear to be giving in to pressure to allow them greater and greater roles. In the brief space we have here, then, let us see if we can hold this issue up to the Word of God and view it as clearly and honestly as possible.

In the New Testament, which contains God's detailed instructions for his church, it would indeed seem, on first glance, that the matter is fairly clear regarding women and ministry. Those who would be elders in the church must be men; in addition, women are not allowed to "teach or exercise authority" over them (1 Tim 2:12). Paul's reasoning is simple: the created order shows that God intended men to have this leadership role, which extends to the family life (Eph 5:22–24). However, other textual evidence makes the matter a bit less certain. As has been noted by many, it seems women occupied the role of prophetess in the early days of the church (Acts 21:9, 1 Cor 11:5); Paul's only admonition in the context of the latter verse is to make sure women pray or prophesy with a symbol of authority on their heads (verse 5ff). And then there is the matter of deacons; the somewhat cryptic 1 Timothy 3:11 may refer to deaconesses, and not deacon's wives, which has caused some Evangelical churches to open up the office of deacon to women.

Thus, while Paul's teaching on the matter seems clear, there seem to be exceptions in the Scriptural record, though not outright contradictory evidence. It is certainly beyond the scope of this book, again, to dive deeply into these matters; suffice it to say, I believe Paul's teaching on women as found in such passages as 1 Timothy 2:12 to be normative for the church, as the majority of Evangelical theologians have concluded.[5] Paul's general teaching of the authority of men over women is too pervasive, too clearly stated, and too firmly rooted in creation to be dismissed by either appeals to culture, context, or similar concerns. So what more might there be to add on this issue? I have two concerns that have been mentioned by many others, but which are well worth repeating here, and should serve to greatly caution anyone who wishes to see changes on this issue.

First of all, it is certainly no small matter that such challenges to traditional Christian belief—and make no mistake, the view above has certainly been part of orthodox Christian teaching since the beginning[6]—are occurring as part of larger trends within the secular culture. In other words, they are not trends first from within the church; they are trends from without. The roots of feminism run back at least to the 1700s in our culture, as is well known, and find early expression in such works as Mary Wollstonecraft's historic *A Vindication of the Rights of Woman*, published in 1792, which was primarily aimed at arguing for the importance of female education, as any good high school history class will tell you. And while we would certainly agree with many of the aims and arguments of such early works, which corrected imbalances that had persisted for centuries, we would certainly not agree with more recent trends, which seek to argue, for example, for no differences at all in roles between men and women. The point is that such trends have been part of a larger

---

5. For a defense of this position, see Moo, "What Does It Mean," 233–52.
6. Again, see Moo, "What Does it Mean," 233.

movement in a culture that has gradually lost its spiritual moorings and sought to replace traditional Christian teaching on a variety of subjects with a vastly different agenda. Questioning all sorts of moral traditions has long been the spirit of the age. Indeed, all of intellectual history in the modern era could be described as a struggle to detach itself from Christianity. We are now far downstream from such movements. Are we seriously going to consider and allow into the church every trend from such a culture?

There is no doubt that imbalances will always need to be sought out and corrected. Women have certainly suffered abuses over the years, even stemming from the incorrect application of certain biblical texts. I have known professing Christian men in Reformed churches that have not even allowed their wives and daughters to speak without permission. Such abuses are no doubt far more disgusting to our Lord than they are even to us! I have also been in contexts where it is taught that a woman's only role is to be a wife and mother. Surely this too is wrong; Jesus calls all to follow him in giving their lives up for his mission first and foremost. But to make changes that have their roots in a culture that has long since moved away from Christian teaching is a dangerous and foolhardy enterprise. Even supposed Evangelicals today are spending great amounts of time and energy pursuing possible ways in which biblical tradition can be questioned and overturned. It seems to be the favorite thing among the younger generation of professing Christians. But surely one remedy to this problem is a sober glance backward.

Another thing that is greatly troubling is the current state of the Evangelical church. As we have said repeatedly in this book, there is such little understanding of and obedience to the call of Christ to discipleship, which demands a surrender of all that we are to the will of Christ, and such a generally *unspiritual* atmosphere in the church, with its lack of serious emphasis on sin, the holiness of God, the Holy Spirit, prayer, and the like, that I am strongly tempted to see such recent trends as the one under consideration in the worst possible light: as a movement completely devoid of the Spirit of God. As I have already said, we live in a time of rampant ambition, characterized by, among other things, relentless attempts at self-promotion. I have now come to the realization during my time in the States that this is a particularly pernicious problem among white middle-class people, and this includes white middle-class women. There is a restlessness among this class of Christians that causes them to seek leadership roles, ministry opportunities, etc., without even a hint, it seems, of the godly preparation we have discussed. This is, indeed, an age of self-promotion. I would say this on the matter: before the Evangelical church makes any decisions, or comes to any conclusions, about adopting any sort of new policies, or even expanding ways in which women can be involved in the church, it had better come to grips with its own lack of spirituality and its problem of earthly ambition.

If a truly godly, mature woman who has had years of proven character, who has not actively sought any position or engaged in any degree of self-promotion, should be granted an occasion to speak to the church, men included; if such a woman has been granted the gift of genuine spiritual insight, especially after years of service to the Lord; if such a woman is endowed with Christ-worthy humiliation; then certainly there are occasions where she might so speak, though I must add it should not be from a position of authority in the church, and it should not be in an acknowledged teaching capacity. Indeed, let her encourage or even exhort the church as a whole, men included. I have sat under many such women on numerous and varied occasions. But where are such women in the church today? In fact, where are such men? If the aforementioned standards were applied to men as well, no doubt we would have far fewer teachers in the church today. Indeed, we would all rather sit under a mature, godly woman than a young, immature, untested man any day; or so I hope. Maleness may be a necessary condition for holding a church office, but it is certainly not a sufficient one. The main issue here, again, is a spiritual one. But we must also remain faithful to the clear teaching of the Bible, which places clear limits on the role of women in the church.

There were indeed prophetesses in the New Testament, and apparently they did pass on inspired messages to the church (1 Cor 11:5). But are we seriously going to argue that the church is in such a Spirit-saturated state today as the early church was? If such occasions are to arise when the Lord inspires a woman to exhort men, it had better indeed be the work of the Holy Spirit of God himself. But in this cool, hip, trendy, shallow, pop-oriented, self-centered, world-saturated, unholy, unspiritual age of Evangelicalism in which we live, where we can all hardly spend five minutes in Spirit-empowered prayer, where we are completely untested, unproven, unsanctified spiritual neophytes, who know nothing of real sacrifice, humility, maturity, and holiness, are we seriously going to pay attention to and be unduly influenced by such cultural trends? How absurd.

Let God's will and word stand. It has often been observed that the women most eager to gain the spotlight are those who, in fact, are least worthy of it. Away with such foolish ambition. If Christian women, and indeed Christian men, are to be used of God in any ministry, or wish to be, let them first seek to trod the old paths. Let such women learn to be submissive, supportive servers of God, husband, and family. Let them learn to exude real spiritual character. Let them serve in prayer, charity, mutual encouragement, etc. Let them seek ways to get directly involved with the mission of God. Away with the seeking of platforms and public ministry—men and women included. This epidemic of ambition, I contend, is the real enemy here. When we learn to truly submit ourselves to the will of God, and humble ourselves under his mighty hand, then he will indeed place us where he wants at the proper time. The Evangelical church had better guard against this and other trends with all their might until it gets itself back on track. Above all, what we need are men and women truly seeking God in prayer, with all their hearts. Then, perhaps, will the Spirit give real direction on this and other critical issues.

7

The Way Forward

So many unforgettable things happened during my brief time on the mission field. A lifetime passed in those seven years. Living in another culture added a certain luminescence to my daily life, no doubt due to reasons that were ultimately self-serving. But I also experienced death as I never had before and never would again. I saw suffering and tragedy on a scale I had scarcely imagined. I was also confronted with spiritual warfare to a degree I hadn't yet known, though it is true that I have known such since. But to this day, the sights and sounds, the encounters and the emotions, the successes, and mostly, the failures, haunt my memory like specters come for reckoning. It's taken years to get over some of it; much of it I'll likely never get over. Sin and death come easily in third-world countries; real progress, spiritual or otherwise, comes slowly, with literal blood, sweat, and tears. The task of missions indeed remains urgent—but it is not an easy one.

A final story illustrates both points. One quiet afternoon in the country where we worked, during my first stint on the field, a telephone call alerted us to a pending police investigation of foreigners and their apartments. Having been warned of such visits but never having experienced them, panic drove us into something of a frenzy. On my father's orders, I began burning copies of sensitive material in my bedroom window; there wasn't any other place to do it. When the stacks of papers steadfastly refused to light, I grabbed a hair dryer from the bathroom and began to focus gusts of air on the dimly-lit pages. Rather than feed the fire, however, the sudden blasts blew it completely out—and the still-legible fragments completely out the window.

Up, up in the air they flew in a cloud of white, then down they fluttered, together at first, then gradually fanning out in various directions as they caught the breeze. It seemed like they would stay aloft forever; our apartment was on the top floor. I watched in horror as the fragments eventually wafted over the entire complex. I had been sent to destroy the evidence; I had now disseminated proof of our crimes to every available witness. Things were not going well.

Nothing seemed to come of my foolishness, thankfully, but we still had mountains of evidence to get rid of. Bibles, commentaries, study guides, Sunday school materials—these were too valuable to get rid of, so my parents elected to hide them. But where? Eventually someone suggested a remote countryside location. We could bury the materials out there, wait a while, and then, when the danger had passed, return to pick them up. One morning soon after, my father and his faithful translator packed up the trusty 4x4 and headed out of town in the silent darkness of the early morning hours. Eventually turning onto an unassuming dirt road and driving away from the highway a bit, they stopped at a nice grassy spot amid a grove of trees. There they dug a large hole in the soft earth and buried the crate of materials, covering the area with loose dirt and making it appear as undisturbed as possible. They then returned to town safe and sound, with no one the wiser.

A few months passed, and the fearful visit never came. Thinking it safe to retrieve the materials, my father and his translator piled back in the jeep again and headed out of town. Day had begun to break by the time they drew near the site. As they rounded the final bend before the dirt road turn-off, they saw something that to this day makes their hair stand on end. Dozens of police vehicles and army trucks were scattered all around the dirt road opening, and government personnel were everywhere. In the still dim light, they somehow managed to squeeze past the commotion and continue down the road apparently undetected; after a while they pulled off the road and waited.

What were they to do? After remaining parked for a considerable period of time, they decided to return and see if the drama had passed and the cars were gone. As they crept around the corner toward the scene, they were horrified to find that it was still very much in progress. Uncertain of what to do, they slowed the vehicle—but it was too late.

They had clearly been spotted. A member of the military was waving them forward. Hearts pounding, they pulled up to the scene. A guard asked them tersely what they were doing there.

After stammering out a reply, an attempt at both honesty and secrecy—a delicate line we walked frequently in that country—they were told to wait. Fearing the worst, they sat completely still, hearts still racing, mouths dry, in the now full morning sun. The seconds passed slowly. *What in the world was going on?* The possibility was clearly strong that their materials had been discovered, but what was taking so long? Would military personnel be returning to interview them, or, worse, haul them off to prison? We had just begun our work in that country; would it now be over after only a year or so?

As these thoughts went through their minds, another large truck pulled up to the scene, turning halfway in the highway and then backing up to the opening to the dirt road. *What in the world was this?* they wondered. Then, as if in a dream, from the back of the covered truck bed men began to descend. Not military personal this time, but dirty, ragged men, their hands tied securely behind their backs. Guards began to file out with them, this time with rifles. As my father and his translator watched in growing horror, the guards began to lead the ragged group down the dirt road. The march was deliberate, methodical, and unmistakably ominous. Soon the group disappeared from sight.

As my father and his translator stared at each other breathlessly, the inevitable happened. A volley of rifle shots exploded through the vacant atmosphere like claps of thunder. Then, sure enough, back they came—only this time, the ragged band were being carried, one by one, and unceremoniously dumped into the truck bed like so many bags of garbage, their lifeless bodies covered carelessly in bloody blankets. As if handling a delivery, the military personnel hopped back into the truck and rumbled off. The remaining guards emerged from the dirt road, got into their own cars, and left. The last personnel man waved my father and his translator through. They didn't speak for miles.

When I met them for lunch that day, as we had previously planned, their faces were ghostly white, and their voices trembled. I couldn't remember when I had seen my father so shaken. As they relayed the story to me, it was almost impossible to take in. Clearly, we had somehow managed to bury our materials directly on a site the government used for mass executions, which were rather common in that country. We had avoided detection, perhaps—nothing short of a miracle—but to witness the brutality of what unfolded that morning had shaken my father and his translator to their core. It was many more months before they were brave enough to once again return to the scene and attempt to retrieve their materials, this time in the middle of the night. Sure enough, the crate was still there, buried and undisturbed in the same location. Only this time, there were bullet casings scattered around the area, clearly visible in the beam of their flashlights.

I often return to this episode in my memory. Few stories from our time there better illustrate the urgency and difficulty of the task at hand. The initial security scare rattled us, and it alerted us to the dangers of working in that country. But to have such a tragic scene play out on the very spot we had chosen to hide our materials was almost more than we could wrap our minds around. For me, the lesson lingers. These matters are deadly serious. Time is wasting. People all around the world are dying. Life is cheap in many countries. That pitiful band of men—criminals, to be sure, but no less deserving of God's grace and truth than any of us—had any of them ever heard the gospel? Based on what we knew of that country, it was unlikely. We were on an urgent mission, indeed, but on that day these men were completely out of reach—only inches away from the very message we had brought to give them hope. As they fell to the ground that day, their lifeblood seeping into the clean earth, down through the layers of sand, perhaps, to the very pages and words that might have saved them utterly, the irony could not have been thicker. Never, perhaps, had such desperate souls been so close to salvation, a salvation they never even knew they needed. And never so far away.

AN ENCOURAGEMENT

In this book I have attempted to set forth as clearly as possible some basic but essential elements of practical Christianity, elements that, in my view, very much need to be freshly and fully apprehended by the modern church. I started with the gospel, seeking to establish with certainty the old Reformation gospel, the gospel of justification by faith. However, I also sought to establish the necessary doctrine of discipleship, the call of Jesus to all souls to leave everything and follow him. Again, these doctrines have been well-defended in recent decades, but perhaps often not with enough nuance and care. I then sought to apply several aspects of discipleship to the Christian life directly, paying special attention to ambition, that critical driving force in the human soul that Jesus calls us clearly to fully lay down in following him. We then looked at several more crucial areas of holiness before moving on to discuss perhaps the two most critical needs in the church today, prayer and the Holy Spirit. We then sought to examine some areas in which the church today is, perhaps, failing to properly set forth the notion of mission, or to properly understand the significance of ministry. We then turned our attention to the great American idol of politics, before finishing with some comments on how the church should rightly approach the various causes that are the occasion of so much discord both in society and in the church.

In this final chapter, I hope to make some very practical final suggestions about how the church should seek to move forward on all these matters. Before we do that, however, a few follow-up comments on the previous chapters are in order. First of all, I think it needs to be said again that in making many of the observations and comments I have made, I am not in any way seeking to be overly critical or judgmental. I stand as much in need of what I have said here as anyone; this much is certain. But to the modern Christian, some of what I have said here may sound harsh or even condemnatory. Much of the Evangelical world is not used to straightforward language, to be sure. But my contention here has been that these are Jesus's words, not mine. These are his demands, not the demands of a cynical onlooker. I have sought here to faithfully present the teachings of Jesus as clearly as possible, but I have indeed also pointed out places where I believe the church is failing. We must not shrink from critical inquiry or self-examination. It is through this, and only this, that change can be made. Proper treatment cannot commence without an accurate diagnosis of the malady.

But perhaps, here at the end, some further clarifications are in order. I have made the rather strong statement that if Jesus's call to discipleship is not clearly and definitely preached to lost sinners, there is a danger that one may not be responding to the full gospel as Jesus presented it, and thus might be in danger of not being truly saved. There has indeed been a temptation among some writers on these issues to present discipleship as a subsequent step in the whole process of following Jesus: first, one is saved by faith, and then one gradually learns to be a disciple. But the problems here are obvious, and have been thoroughly pointed out by many. The first problem is that this is simply not how Jesus presented the matter. As we have seen, discipleship is a necessary aspect of coming to Jesus at all. The other problem is that it can make discipleship seem optional for the Christian. But clearly it is not. Only disciples of Jesus enter heaven. And as we have seen, the apostles as well present things in this manner; following Jesus requires us both to pursue and to some degree achieve all that Jesus commanded. It is life in the Holy Spirit that leads to salvation, even if it is not the ground or cause of it.

But some may protest that they were saved simply by coming to a fresh awareness of their sin, being broken over it in real repentance, and clinging to the Savior as their only hope. The full demands of following Christ, perhaps, were only later fully apprehended. And here, I think, we can offer some agreement. Let us be clear: I do not believe that anyone can be a true Christian without having at least some real understanding of what following Jesus in full surrender really means. No one truly comes to Christ without a conception of him as their Lord; without a real appreciation, however incomplete, that they are submitting to him in real and full obedience. This is undeniably what following Jesus involves. But often this understanding is, in fact, incomplete. Again, the very concept of repentance, I contend, as well as a true understanding of the person of Christ, demands that we come to him with full submission and surrender. But certainly most of us, if not all of us, have no clear or extensive notion of what this truly means, especially when we are first converted. It is an undeniable truth of Christian experience that our God has in store for us levels of humility, purity, growth, surrender, and dedication to him that we never even dreamed of! The disciples followed Jesus willingly, but still could not have apprehended the horrors of Jesus's arrest, trial, and execution. Paul could not anticipate how cold the prison shackles would feel, nor James the sharpness of sword. In essence, we simply don't know where Jesus will lead us. I would add that growth in the laying down of one's life in real surrender takes time, like growth in any grace. There is and indeed must be a full and complete willingness in coming to Christ—again, he preached the demands of total surrender at the outset, to all who came to him—but there is no question, again, that often we don't know what we are getting into. We are willing, but woefully ignorant. The path of true discipleship is inevitably one in which God takes us deeper and deeper into our own ignorance, superficiality, and pride, and gradually transforms us more and more into the image of Jesus.

And yet I repeat my claim that the call of Christ to discipleship must be fully and unapologetically preached—and today more than ever, with comfort and compromise being the order of the day. Much of the Evangelical church is so far removed from its true roots it is almost laughable, if it wasn't so disgraceful. The Evangelical church today is either, it seems sometimes, merely an activist organization devoid of any spiritual knowledge, holiness, and power on the one hand, in danger of caving completely to culture; or a sincere but superficial and immature group of spiritual novices on the other, who talk of things like the gospel but have no real grace or power in their lives. Many of the latter camp are the ones that fill the huge but somehow still growing mega-churches in the South today, the ones with fancy merchandise and customer-service packages, can't-miss weekend worship experiences, and young, hip, pastors who get their sermons prepared by professional research organizations—and not, apparently, by the Holy Spirit working within them (so much for drawing forth from one's treasure things new and old). Such churches often draw people in, but in my mind, unless the full call of Christ to discipleship is preached, as well as the full realities of sin, holiness, and biblical doctrine, we are in grave danger of merely collecting lapsed cultural Christians.

I have witnessed what appear to be genuine testimonies in such churches, and I do believe some are being saved; but I also know that the more we compromise the truth to reach people, the greater the danger is that we will have false conversions—converts, but not disciples. In the South especially, these churches have baptisms seemingly every week, but whether these are genuine or not, God only knows. It is quite easy, I have found, to generate "decisions," especially in the gospel-saturated South. It is common, for example, for young people raised in Christian homes to undergo conversion experiences as part of the normal process of growing up; but the question from Jesus is, who will follow him truly and to the end? We hold to the doctrine of justification by faith with all our hearts, and we believe in radical conversions. But as theologians have become increasingly aware, salvation must be presented as involving a "narrow gate" and a "narrow way," the only path that leads to eternal life, as Jesus presented it. Let us recall again that salvation is often presented in the Bible as being at the end of the path, not the beginning. Thus, I contend again that the church had better give up its seeker-friendly methods once and for all, or its presentation of cheap grace, and beware of compromising in the name of contextualization. God is not calling groupies to a church brand; he is not looking for tolerant sympathizers. He is calling disciples to die to themselves and follow him. The difference is eternal life itself.

But there is encouragement here as well; salvation is not won or lost in the middle of the journey either. My friend, have you fallen into sin? Pick yourself up and keep going on the path. Are you discouraged? Look to the end, where Jesus beckons. Are you unsure whether you are a true disciple? Here is an unfailing sign: *whether you keep on going or not.* The true Christian doesn't perfect himself, or always defeat sin. The true Christian *keeps on going*. He may not always be able to see his progress, but he *keeps on going*. He may wonder sometimes if he is even on the path; but inside and out, he *keeps on going*. And just at the last, when he feels, perhaps, the sudden pangs of overwhelming fear and guilt, so much so that he begins to waver right at the very door of heaven, a divinely-cloaked arm will reach out from behind the gate and pull him in to safety. It's all God, my friends, all the time. If you are a true Christian, he will *keep you going*. The last sin will one day be *the last sin*. Your next step *will* be holiness. You *will* cut off right hands and pluck out right eyes. You *will* maintain the standard of holiness you have attained (Phil 3:16). You *will* continue at the altar of prayer. And you *will* be used by God for good in this world. There was a time in my life, many times in fact, when I thought I was gone for sure, or at least beyond the boundary of usefulness for God. But his faithfulness has always prevailed. We are his very work; he will see us through, for the glory of his name.

A NEW VISION FOR UNITY: IS IT POSSIBLE?

I have wondered for some time what would happen if different Evangelical denominations came together for nothing but intercessory prayer. I am still waiting for this to happen. We have shown a willingness to come together for missions or theological conferences, and for the gospel's sake; but what good are these without prayer? Jonathan Edwards saw the need of it, years ago;[1] and our churches are in a far worse state, without question, than those in his day could ever fear to be. Even the Evangelical church is rife with idols, immorality, covetousness, and worldliness the likes of which Edwards never dreamed of. How far we have fallen in our day; and we are all affected. How foolish to suppose that we are gaining any ground against the spiritual forces of evil, on the mission field or even here at home, without a real and persistent dedication to prayer, the one activity that the Bible says is our greatest hope in the battle. The time has come for unity, even if our doctrine, churches, and ministries remain separate. We must unite in prayer. It remains our only hope.

---

1. I am referring here, of course, to his "A Call to United, Extraordinary Prayer."

I would love to see prayer conferences spring up all over the country. Keep preaching out of it. We have enough preaching at present. Keep doctrine out of it. We have more than enough doctrine to live for God. And keep even "worship" out of it. Too many prayer times turn into the beat-driven, sensual entertainment fests we like to call worship. Get people together to do nothing but prayer, for at least a solid hour. And do it again. And again. And if the devil knocks one or two people down, others must fill their spots, and rise to the occasion. There is strength in numbers, and we will need large numbers to defeat this enemy.

But is there any hope for greater unity, even around prayer? It would seem unlikely. The issue of baptism alone is keeping Protestants apart. Am I willing to put differences aside for greater fellowship, prayer, and practice with those who differ over baptism or other matters? I certainly did on the mission field; it is fascinating how being on the front lines, in hostile territory, teases unity out of the most narrow-minded among us. Unity happens there because it must. Survival is at stake. Let us then remain in our separate churches if we must. But can we not come together to pray, witness, and do acts of charity, at least from time to time? Can we not begin really to fellowship together? How bizarre it is that we cannot. The world is not impressed with us; it cannot be affected by us; for we do not yet demonstrate that unity that shows the world that our Lord is who he claimed to be (John 17:21). Pitifully, we are even dividing over earthly things, things that don't even matter, such as political opinions. How disgraceful.

In at least one sense, however, there should not be unity. I have become convinced that Evangelical mega-churches, especially those built on brands or cults of personality, should be broken up. Having spent time in several of these, I have witnessed the shallowness, the lack of significant doctrine, the total absence of shepherding, and the misplaced priorities in general. The Evangelical world is massing together, but not around the right things. I am not saying it is all bad—the best of these mega churches are at least attempting to love others and evangelize their communities and the world. But they are doing so without real power. And church members themselves are not growing. People are not being fed. The pastors that are being put in place in these churches are often young, untested, unproven, and hopelessly inexperienced. To call on them to shepherd these growing masses is absurd. And these churches inevitably move into places where other healthy churches already exist and take them over, like so many large corporations taking over local businesses, as it is often said. It really is absurd and deeply wrong. Of course you can attract more people if you have the means to put on a better show and offer a better product, if you will. But professing Christians who are drawn to these inevitably get lost or thrown into the small-group system, that great catch-all that large churches depend on to do their shepherding. I see the significance of frequent fellowship and interaction with other believers in the New Testament; the body is indeed called to "build itself up in love" (Eph 4:16). But this is not the same thing as shepherding, which is the very serious calling of God's pastors (1 Pet 5:2). Honestly, I have yet to attend a small-group that did anything of much use. Usually they devolve into bland Bible studies. If anything, they should be used for prayer, and again, not for shepherding. But they should certainly not be forced upon congregations to make allowances for pastoral staffs that are pressed beyond their limits. I believe fellowship and prayer groups should be encouraged, but should perhaps happen organically. At most, brothers and sisters at the same stage in life, or who have struggles in common, should come together and minister to each other. But the point here, again, is that churches are simply too big today. Small groups often exist essentially for this reason, and this is truly unfortunate.

THE NEEDS OF THE WORLD RECONSIDERED: GOD WILL NOT BE RUSHED

In a previous chapter, we considered the state of missions in the world today. There is no question that although the world has been evangelized to some extent, its larger needs are as glaring as ever. With the rise of new media outlets like the Internet, the world has more advantages, perhaps, than it ever has since the very beginning of Christianity; but there are still large pockets of people who have not heard a clear presentation of the gospel. As an aside, in my experience with missions I have never been quite convinced of the need to focus strictly on people groups; I believe the Bible's division of "people, tribe, nation and tongue" to be largely a figurative statement, denoting completeness.[2] Indeed, practically speaking, my experience overseas, working in areas with a large number of people groups, led me to believe that there was ample distribution of representatives of those groups in the larger population to counterbalance

---

2. Consider, for example, Mark 16:15, which compels us to preach the gospel to "all creation."

the rather extreme focus we have in our day on specific, tiny pockets of people. Though we don't have time to search it out, it seems clear that the emphasis of both Christ and the apostle Paul—after the poor and needy, who get the gospel first in Christ's ministry—was on those who haven't heard; and to me, it seems that the greatest number of such people who haven't heard still needs to be prioritized. Of course, access to the gospel is paramount; but I have known missionaries who have spent their whole lives trying to minister to tiny pockets of people in the name of people groups, while unaware that close and near relatives of these groups were scattered throughout the much larger population they were ignoring. I learned this specifically in the country in which I worked, where we worked both in the countryside and in large cities where students from remote places were gathering. What seems to me to be the problem here is that there exists, for some inexplicable reason, a bias toward people groups in missions today, that obviously developed in the last fifty years in Evangelicalism; but I remain skeptical of its solid foundations, both biblically and practically.

But these strategic questions aside, the needs of the world are still great, and urgent; yet I repeat my concerns about inadequate methodology. The work of God, quite simply, cannot be rushed. The making of a man of God takes time. This is the biblical pattern. And these are the ones upon whom God pours his anointing. I am therefore puzzled and rather grieved over the Evangelical world's attempts to engage in strategies that downplay or even completely ignore what is essentially God's method: proven men, prepared, called, and anointed by God, to go and plant churches in needy places. One man raised up by God in this way is truly worth a thousand who are not. Again, I am not saying that this is all there is to missions. My mother, for example, and many like her, have headed up charity operations that carry on this essential and critically-needed aspect of the mission of Christ with great spiritual blessing, and such endeavors have also opened up vast opportunities for the gospel. Indeed, all those who wish to follow Christ, as we have said, must commit themselves to carrying out his mission first and foremost, and this includes women, children, and all those not engaged in full-time ministry. But such must come alongside the man of God and the church-planting endeavor in support, especially in prayer. And while many Evangelical churches have at least some notion of this biblical pattern, the standards for meeting it seem incredibly low.

Again, the church must begin again to take a robust and active role in raising such people up and overseeing them, and they need to begin to take the issue of spiritual maturity far more seriously. Training cannot be given over to missions agencies; such people are not called by God to train others. This is for those already gifted by God to engage in such ministries themselves. The biblical record shows this clearly (2 Tim 2:2). Again, the Reformed community got this largely right. It all comes down to God himself and his Spirit, and, again, his work cannot be rushed. If there is one thing I did learn, both in myself and in others I observed overseas, it is that God is not going to use people in any significant way without his anointing on their lives. There is a very real sense in which God doesn't need any particular person to do his work! And his highest calling for us is not, contrary to what Southern Baptists teach, that we do evangelism. His primary concern, I am convinced, is that we be holy in character: humble, pure, empty of self, delighting in him, and loving others. Certainly, if one wishes to claim so, caring for others in evangelism and love is part of the character he wishes to build within us; it is, without question, one of the most prominent attributes of our Lord Jesus himself. But my point here is that in terms of ministry, the work is the Lord's, and he is going to use those he has prepared to be vessels of his Holy Spirit. 2 Timothy 2:19-22 makes this abundantly clear. God's purpose for his ministers is that they first be cleansed. Then they will be useful to the master for service.

We must, then, wait upon the Lord in humble prayer. Christian leaders today talk of many things, but prayer occupies a tragically small part of their message. The Evangelical church will continue to be a mile wide and an inch deep, spiritually-speaking, until God continues to mold and fashion its priorities. Until the church today spends hours and hours in slow and painstaking prayer, depending on God for every leading, and waiting until the answers come from him, the results we see, in our own country or abroad, will continue the current dangerous trend—this trend of shallow Christianity, this trend of careless doctrine and reckless practice, this powerless, far too unholy, and largely ineffectual tide of youthful exuberance that characterizes the church today; this movement that is yet to know anything, I am afraid, of real sacrifice or spiritual warfare, of battles with real supernatural forces won or lost on the efficacy of prayer.

My hope is that the leaders of the Evangelical world, and the New Calvinism movement in particular, will one day come to understand this principle personally; and that God is preparing many such leaders for the real work of missions, so that one day they will be called by God to leave their worlds of comfort and success for the far more difficult work of giving one's life and soul to the breaking of hard, dry ground. Even practically speaking, we cannot send primarily short-termers and businessmen to the front lines to do this work; what a laughable strategy. We must send the best of us—the most mature, most gifted, most Spirit-anointed, most battle-ready and battle-hardened, who are prepared not merely to give their lives, but to give what is far less glorious but often much harder—a lifetime of soul-draining service. I am presently waiting on God to make me such a person, and to return me to the front lines if he wills; until then, may we as Christians take up that other work of missions, the work to which the vast majority of us are called—the work of prayer. And then, in a prevailing atmosphere of "ministering to the Lord and fasting" (Acts 13:2–3), may God show us whom he will set aside to that most serious of all callings, the work of the ministry.

WHAT THE PANDEMIC SHOWED

In my view, the ongoing coronavirus pandemic has revealed just how far the Evangelical church has to go in terms of heavenly-mindedness. I am not denying how challenging it has been for everyone; we have all failed, in some capacity, to honor God through this difficulty. Some of us were overly anxious; others overly insensitive. In the very beginning especially, it was enormously difficult even to tell what the truth of the matter was. But when the situation began to escalate, and the media started to report large numbers of deaths, the Evangelical church, in my view, began to fail. Partly fueled by loyalty to the political administration that was then in office, American Evangelicals allowed their obsession with an "us vs. them" mentality toward anything they view as "liberal" to become so exacerbated that many of them simply refused to take the growing crisis seriously. It got bizarre almost beyond understanding. Christians were denying the reality of the virus altogether, or, more commonly, simply refusing to wear a mask. What this amounted to, in my view, was a complete failure to love one's neighbor. Consideration was not given to the elderly or otherwise most vulnerable; the benefit of the doubt was not at all given to those who took the virus seriously. Surely, if even a few people in our communities were vulnerable—truly vulnerable—the church would act with the utmost care and consideration, right? Sadly, no. Identifying largely with the Right—or at least appearing to—many in the church simply refused to go along with anything reported in the media. It was an incredible opportunity for the church to shine the love of Jesus. And it failed. Miserably.

There is no need, of course, to revisit the issue in detail, except to make a few additional observations. First of all, is our mistrust of the media so great that we refuse what seems obvious? Even if the dangers of the virus were slightly exaggerated at some point, what one had to conclude to avoid taking the virus seriously was that *every single government and media outlet in every single country that reported major fatalities* was somehow in on a giant conspiracy. Or, that somehow every major scientist in every single country that reported these things was somehow duped into thinking the virus was killing people. The liberal media in America wasn't to blame; all the liberal medias in all the countries were. All the stories, all the pictures, and all the reports were simply lies.

Yes, some perhaps thought, the virus kills some people, but only the elderly or very weak. But this kind of thinking only makes the church seem more insensitive. Jesus came to love and protect the weakest among us. How perverted that we should not care for them—and indeed for every living soul. The only proper attitude toward this pandemic, in light of our call to love our neighbors as ourselves, was to take it with the utmost seriousness, and strive to let the world know that we care. Wear a mask, if it might slow the virus's spread? I will gladly wear a mask. I will wear one all the time and without complaint. Social distancing? Gladly. Vaccine? If it can help save lives, I will at least seriously consider it.

I am not saying, again, that the situation wasn't difficult. I understand that people are mistrusting of the media. I understand that the economic effects of the pandemic were disastrous for some. But surely we can't get so sideways in our thinking that we forget our calling in the world. What an incredible shame that the unbelieving world often manifests more concern for needy people than the church! I heard the most bizarre things said by Christians during this time. I even heard Christians say that their freedom not to wear a mask was more important than any health concern. Again, for so many professing Christians it often comes down to freedom and economic interests—those twin idols that the American church is so willingly serving. God have mercy on us. My family personally knew three church elders who died from the virus. A family friend, a young husband and father, died tragically of COVID as well. Others I know were hospitalized and went through hellish experiences. I know many in other countries that continue to struggle mightily against the virus, especially poor countries. And yes, economic considerations were important. But in my view, the medical establishment—which was ordained by God to handle these issues at the present time—did the best they could do. Again, in this case at least, they seemed to value human life more than many Christians! To so many Evangelicals, apparently, *nothing* seems to matter more than their own interests.

Nor did I understand, frankly, some churches' insistence on gathering together throughout the pandemic. To me, again, this felt like insensitivity of the highest order. The virus was clearly capable of making anyone seriously sick, and of killing the elderly and vulnerable. The only way to justify meeting during this time, it seems to me, was to completely reject the reality of the pandemic. Which is what many Evangelical pastors vocally and publicly did. I confess I didn't understand this at all. What may be missing here, again, is a true understanding of how the compassion of Christ is an essential element of his mission. It could be argued from the gospel accounts that such tangible, visible expressions of love should absolutely lead the way in our dealings with unbelievers. They should at least mark us out as followers of Christ. They should be distinguishing marks of our faith. They should identify us *overwhelmingly*. But of course they do not. We have no idea how to "weep with those who weep." We have little conception as an Evangelical church of how to sympathize, emphasize, reach out for others, care for others, consider others, etc. We have so little of the actual emotional life of Christ as represented in the gospels that it is frightening. And the pandemic revealed all of that. It became, again, another chapter in the "us vs. them" political, earthly feud that the American Evangelical church is somehow engrossed in. It should have showed how detached from worldly concerns we are, how we can recognize when real need is present and rise above feelings of distrust and discontentment with the world and be the visible hands and feet of Jesus. But it didn't. It simply revealed what I have pointed out all along in this book: how utterly un-Christlike we all are. One close pastor friend of my father's told me on the phone that he feels the church "has blood on its hands" because of its behavior during the pandemic. I can't help but agree. God forgive us.

IT'S NOW OR NEVER

As Evangelicals, we have a church that is, in general, attempting to hold on to doctrines, at least, that have long since slipped away in non-Evangelical contexts; but what we should be holding onto more than anything else is the hem of the garment of our risen Lord in unfailing prayer. The Lord told us to keep on praying, so that our God will answer us in time; we have yet even to *begin* this task. Thus, I fear that if greater persecution comes upon the American church, the church will evaporate like the hollow, fragile shell it often appears to be. And that crisis may be right around the corner. Or perhaps it is already upon us.

The church was instructed always to be battle-ready—or, better yet, always to do battle. The foe has never been the lost world—not unbelievers, not "liberals," not the government. The lost world is part of our *mission* as followers of Christ, not our enemies. Our enemies are spiritual, unseen, and hidden. And they are presently winning against the church. I cannot help but conclude so. Again, no one who reads the Bible honestly, and who reads also any good Christian book from any author with any degree of insight from another era, must agree. We are too soft; too weak; too addicted to sensual pleasure and entertainment; too attached to this life; too protective of ourselves; too in love with self-fulfillment; and too utterly unspiritual to maintain any real consistency in prayer. We have no affection for God or real concern for our neighbors. And I include myself here as much as anyone. Is it too late for the Evangelical church?

It is not. Our God is still on the throne, and his power is still what it always was. We speak often of revival, but perhaps we have idolized even it. What we need is simple change, one believer or congregation at a time. Let us not forget that the devotion and holiness that Christ calls us to is precisely what the Holy Spirit, that incredible gift of God to man—that being who is God himself—*longs* to work out in our lives. He longs to fill us to the full with God's grace and power. When that happens, we will be utterly emptied of all thoughts of self; our only thoughts will be of God. We will be drawn to him, unconsciously, involuntarily, and persistently, as our chief and only source of delight; and we will burn with one all-consuming passion to see him glorified in the earth, and to pour out our lives to that end.

My friend, has the Holy Spirit ever flowed from your soul like rivers of living water (John 7:37–39)? Have you ever truly known his real, experiential, glorious power and presence in your life? Has God's love truly been poured into your heart through his Spirit (Rom 5:5)? Have you ever been so strengthened by the Spirit in your inner being that Christ has truly dwelt within you by faith? Have you discovered anything of that unimaginable, inexhaustible reservoir of love that is the very essence of the divine nature (Eph 3:14–19)? Have you ever known anything at all of what it means to be filled with all the fullness of God (verse 19)? Have you known anything at all on earth of the infinitely glorious calling and destiny that is ours? These are the things we must seek, slowly, perhaps, but surely, if there is any hope at all for the glory of God in ourselves, in our churches, and in the world. We must begin to seek the living God—today. The time has come; it's now or never if it ever was.

Bibliography

Akin, Daniel L. and Bruce Riley Ashford. *I Am Going*. Nashville: B&H Publishing, 2016.
"Ambition." *Merriam-Webster Dictionary*. https://www.merriam-webster.com/dictionary/ambition.
Baker, Lynne Rudder. "Why Christians Should Not be Libertarians: An Augustinian Challenge." *Faith and Philosophy* 20.4 (2003) 460–78.
Bonhoeffer, Dietrich. *The Cost of Discipleship*. New York: Touchstone, 1995. Kindle.
Carson, D.A. *Christ and Culture Revisited*. Grand Rapids: Eerdmans, 2012. Kindle.
Cohon, Rachel. "Hume's Moral Philosophy." In *The Stanford Encyclopedia of Philosophy*. Stanford University, 1997–. https://plato.stanford.edu/archives/fall2018/entries/hume-moral/.
Edwards, Jonathan. *Dissertation Concerning The End for Which God Created the World*. https://fourcornerministries.com/wp-content/uploads/2016/09/Edwards-J-13.pdf.
Greear, J.D. *Gospel: Recovering the Power that Made Christianity Revolutionary*. Nashville: B&H, 2011. Kindle.
Hamilton, Jesse. *Prayer: The Church's Great Need*. Sand Springs, OK: Grace and Truth, 2012.
Hart, Matthew J. "Calvinism and the Problem of Hell." In *Calvinism and the Problem of Evil*, edited by David E. Alexander and Daniel M. Johnson, 248–72. Eugene, OR: Wipf and Stock, 2016.
Hauerwas, Stanley and William Willimon. *Resident Aliens*. Nashville: Abingdon Press, 2014. Kindle.
Hume, David. *A Treatise of Human Nature*. Oxford: Clarendon Press, 1896. https://oll.libertyfund.org/title/bigge-a-treatise-of-human-nature#Hume_0213_981.
Kane, Robert. "Libertarianism." In *Four Views on Free Will*, edited by John Martin Fischer, Robert Kane, Derk Pereboom, and Manuel Vargas, 5–43. Oxford: Blackwell, 2007.
Kuyper, Abraham. "Sphere Sovereignty." *Reformational Publishing Project*. Translated by George Kamps. http://www.reformationalpublishingproject.com/pdf_books/Scanned_Books_PDF/SphereSovereignty_English.pdf.
Livius, Titus. *The History of Rome*. Translated by George Baker. Vol 1. New York: Peter A. Mesier, 1823.
MacArthur, John F. *Why Government Can't Save You*. Nashville: Thomas Nelson, 2000.

Moo, Douglas. *James*. Grand Rapids: Eerdmans, 2000.

———. "Israel and the Law in Romans 5–11: Interaction with the New Perspective." In *Justification and Variegated Nomism: The Teaching of Paul*, edited by D. A. Carson, 185–216. Grand Rapids: Eerdmans, 2004.

———. "What Does It Mean Not to Teach or Exercise Authority Over Men." In *Recovering Biblical Manhood and Womanhood*, edited by John Piper and Wayne Grudem, 233–52. Wheaton, IL: Crossway, 2021.

Moreland, J.P. "A Biblical Case for Limited Government." *The Institute for Faith, Work, and Economics*. https://tifwe.org/wp-content/uploads/2013/04/JP-Moreland-Limited-Govt.pdf.

New Oxford American Dictionary. New York: Oxford University Press, 2010.

Piper, John. *God's Passion for His Glory*. Wheaton, IL: Crossway, 1998.

Ravenhill, Leonard. "Zeal: Love Ablaze." *Last Days Ministries*. https://www.lastdaysministries.org/Groups/1000087727/Last_Days_Ministries/Articles/By_Leonard_Ravenhill/Zeal_Love_Ablaze/Zeal_Love_Ablaze.aspx.

The New Encyclopaedia Britannica. 15th ed. 32 vols. Chicago: Encyclopaedia Britannica, 2010. Final print version. Continued online, as *Encyclopaedia Britannica*, at https://www.britannica.com/.

Timpe, Kevin. *Free Will in Philosophical Theology*. New York: Bloomsbury, 2013.

Trotter, Lilias. "Focussed." *Lilias Trotter*. https://ililiastrotter.wordpress.com/out-of-print-manuscripts/.

Truman, Carl. *Republocrat*. Phillipsburg, NJ: P&R, 2010.

Williams, Daniel K. *The Politics of the Cross: A Christian Alternative to Partisanship*. Grand Rapids: Eerdmans, 2021. Kindle.

Wright, Christopher. *The Mission of God*. Downers Grove, IL: IVP Academic, 2006.

www.ingramcontent.com/pod-product-compliance
Lightning Source LLC
Chambersburg PA
CBHW071453150426
43191CB00008B/1330